Rainbow Bears to Make & Collect

by Sally Winey

Published by Hobby House Press
Grantsville, MD 21536
www.hobbyhouse.com

 Dedication

I would like to dedicate the book to my fantastic husband Bill and my three children Chris, Mindy and Abby. They have all given there unconditional love and support to me through out the past 25 years so I could fulfill my dreams.

Cover and Title Page photographs by Beitzel Photography. Photographs by Patty Rowe, Brian White, and Mindy Winey.

Front and Back Cover: Bears made from the "Some Bear from Over the Rainbow" pattern.

Additional copies of this book may be purchased at $19.95 (plus postage and handling)
from
Hobby House Press, Inc.
1 Corporate Drive
Grantsville, Maryland 21536
1-800-554-1447
www.hobbyhouse.com
or from your favorite bookstore or dealer.
©2000 by Sally Winey

Printed in the United States of America

ISBN: 0-87588-593-4

Table of Contents

ACKNOWLEDGEMENTS

I want to thank God for giving me the gifts necessary to do all that I have done and for the great family He gave me. They all equally give of themselves so that I can make the bears and help others to smile. You are the best and I want to thank you for your support. Also for everyone else who has played a part in making it possible for me to bring the love of bear collecting into peoples lives.

Introduction

The fun and enjoyment that bear making has brought into all our lives is immeasurable and sometimes unexplainable. My family has grown up together sharing with others our lives in order to bring you the bears. I am not alone in this process. My husband has dedicated his life to helping me make the bears. He has left several jobs to assist me when the times get rough. He takes care of the kids and me when I must travel and never complains about any of my somewhat crazy ideals. My children also put many hours into helping me make the bears and put up with my requests with cheerful hearts. We have gotten to travel, visit places, meet, touch and be touched by thousands of collectors young and old. We truly love what we do and hope it is an inspiration to all. It seems that we have learned how to lead a rewarding life in the midst of all the chaos around us by pursuing our dreams and not giving up. We have great faith in what we do and a profound hope in a wonderful future with the bears.

In this book, you will see some of my early bears and how, over the years, they have developed and changed. There are "no bad bears" or exact science to making a bear. What counts is the love you put into making him.

I am also sharing with you some of my methods of bear making. The fun of coming up with your own creation is so fulfilling. Then bringing a smile to some- one's face is motivation to make another. I have handmade over 16,000 different bears in the last 18 years and hope to continue making more. All God's love to you and I hope you enjoy the book.

Chapter 1

History of Winey Bears

The first Winey Bear was made in 1983 but the history of Winey Bears goes back even further. I was born Sally Harman and both Grandma Harman and Grandma Martin were very influential in my later development of teddy bears. I spent many wonderful hours sitting by my Grandma Harman as she created patterns for clothing, dolls, and other handcrafted items. These early childhood memories certainly came in handy when I started drawing my very first teddy bear pattern.

One of my earliest memories was that of getting on a bus with my Grandma and traveling to the fabric shops to pick out material for clothing. These trips were a special time of bonding with my Grandmother, but it was also a time of learning the fine art of negotiations. As my Grandmother taught me, there is always the price on the material and then there is the price you pay for the material. These two prices should never be the same. Thus was born the spirit of entrepreneurship within me. Certainly, the need to maintain quality suppliers at reasonable prices would be essential when making hundreds of teddy bears.

After the material was purchased, the real fun began for Grandma and me. Pattern making was the next step in making clothing, and this required plenty of drawing paper and creativity. While Grandma was figuring out just the right shape and size, I was learn-

My little bunny and I at eight months old.

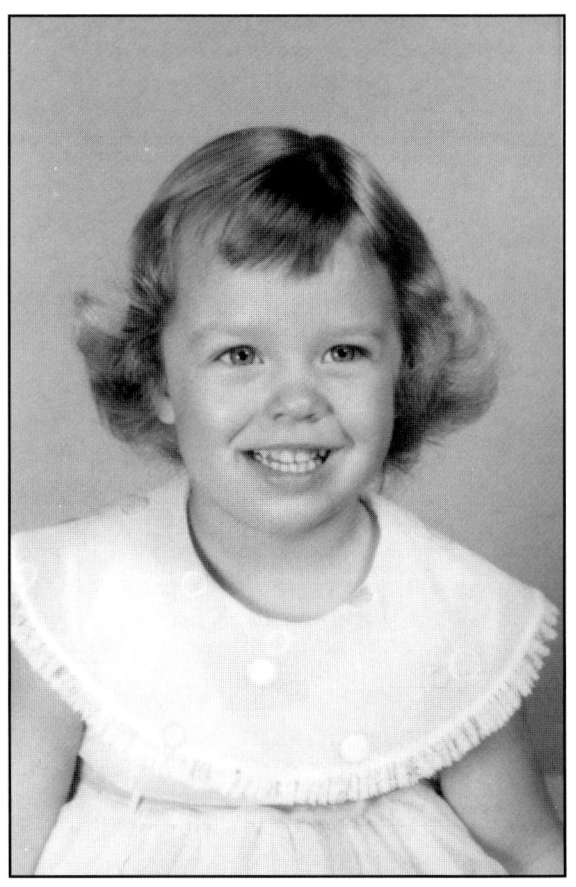

Three years old.

ing all about design. With the creativity in my gene pool, it is no wonder that my designs are considered to be among the most unique Teddy Bears. My first pattern, however, was not for a stuffed animal, but for clothing for me. While my Grandma was designing new clothing, she gave me brown paper bags to use to draw my own pattern for a dress. To this day, I still grab whatever spare piece of paper or napkin I can find to quickly sketch out a new idea. The love I put into each of my creations comes from these very early days of quiet time spent with a loved one. Throughout my early childhood years and continuing through my school age years, I learned and was influenced by my family's creativity. This creativity is found on both sides of my family which, accounts for my strong ability in this area.

My first sewing machine.

When I was ten years old my uncle and I made these puppets at my grandmother's house. I had sewn the clothing while my uncle made the hands and heads.

Bill, Abby, Mindy, Chris and I. 1984.

The next influential period in my life began in 1976 when I married Bill Winey. Without that one single act, there would never have been a Winey Bear. They would have been Harman Bears or Smith or Jones Bears, but certainly not Winey Bears. Bill was trans-ferred to Burlington, IA where we set up our first home. While we were waiting to move into our first apartment, we stayed at the local Holiday Inn. It was there that I met a group of wonderful ladies who, dur-ing their lunch break, taught me how to tat. This is a very intricate process of tying knots to make fancy doilies. I had done some crocheting and knitting in the past but this was totally different. The ladies were amazed that I was even interested in learning how to do this, but when I very quickly caught on to the process, they were very pleased. It seems that virtu-ally no one had any interest in this very lost art form, and these older ladies were delighted to share their secrets with me.

As it turned out, I had plenty of time to practice tatting. I became pregnant with our first child, Christopher, and spent the last four months of my pregnancy on bedrest. We certainly had plenty of decorative table coverings by the time he was born.

A year later we moved to Baltimore, MD where our second child, Mindy, was born. Finally, a girl to make dolls for. Rag dolls, sock dolls, soft sculpture dolls—I made them all for my first daughter. I should have started making bears at that time. I would have gained four more years, but I guess all good things come to those who wait. Four years later, we moved back to Pennsylvania and I had our final child, Abby.

That is when life changed forever. I decided to make my two older children feel special since I was bringing home a new "competitor." I made two small teddy bears, one for Chris and one for Mindy. Since I had limited supplies at that time, I used buttons for the joints and embroidered the eyes, nose, and mouth. I

One of my first mohair bears and is in Joyce Schroeder's collection.

My first bear that I had made for my son Christopher. It has buttons for joints and string for eyes it is 8in (20cm).

Left: *Cord-O-Roy* a manufactured remake of my first bears.

also used what material I had available so the first bear I ever made was done in the very exotic material known as "corduroy." From these first bears came many requests from relatives and friends. I made teddy bears for all my nieces and nephews and for all my friends' children. I made literally hundreds of teddy bears and gave them away before I actually considered selling one.

The first real Teddy Bear Show I ever attended was in Grantville, PA. I remember having to beg Bill and the kids to help me get ready and carry all the props and bears into the hotel where the show was held. If they had realized then how much work would be involved in the future to do shows such as Toy Fair in New York City, I probably would not have convinced them to ever help with the first show. It's interesting how work that builds over a long period of time doesn't seem as overwhelming as it would be if it all came at once. By the time we did our first full booth at Toy Fair, we had already done hundreds of smaller shows that prepared us to some extent for the experience. I still do a minimum of six wholesale shows every year including Toy Fair as well as approximately two dozen retail shows. These shows are scattered around the country and allow me to spend time with collectors on a one on one basis. I think my favorite part of the business is talking to the people that enjoy collecting Teddy Bears.

Winey Bears Studio in St. Peter's Village.

A few years after I started making Teddy Bears, I decided to start my first venture into an actual Teddy Bear shop. A dear friend of mine, Joyce Schroeder, who collected quite a few of my handmade bears helped me setup a shop in the local Farmers Market where there were small spaces available for retail shops. My first shop was very small, but it gave me the opportunity to see exactly what was required to operate a retail business. This would prove to be very valuable information later when my Teddy Bear business became, primarily, a wholesale operation selling to retail shops. I had several starts and restarts in my business as I continued to follow my husband around the country as he got transferred. Each time the business moved we tried to make it a little bigger and a little better. This required a rather large investment in advertising, as it was very important for people to know how to find my bears. Eventually, I found myself in a very picturesque setting in Chester County, Pennsylvania. I finally bought my own place in St. Peters, PA. It was a quaint building in a very historic vil-

lage. This was a beautiful location with only one drawback, no running water. This eventually caused us to sell and relocate to our present location in Morgantown, PA.

The actual business of making Teddy Bears remained virtually unchanged from 1983 to 1998. During that time, the whole process was comprised of my family cutting bears out, dying material, sewing bears, and going to shows to sell them. It was the beginning of 1998 when the whole business changed. I had several articles written about Winey Bears over the years, but in January of 1998, Mary Beth's magazine came out with an article about my history and had a picture of one of my handmade bears. This bear was my trademark style, hand dyed mohair with a very unique pattern. The phone started ringing and just did not stop. When the dust settled, I had so many orders I had to make a decision as to how to proceed. The decision was made to move forward into the arena of manufacturing Winey Bears. We did not want to do this overseas, so we opened our own manufacturing facility right here in the United States. The process remained essentially the same but with more hands to get all the work finished in a timely fashion. We soon realized that the way we always made bears was not efficient if we were going to produce a large quantity of a given pattern. Technology had to come to the handmade bear business. I made two concessions to improve production. The first improvement was a cutting machine that allowed us to cut far more bears with more accuracy than cutting them out by hand. The cutting machine came from an old harness making company and, although it was very old, it really served the purpose and still does to this day. The second improvement was a modern stuffing machine. This machine, coupled with a new air compressor, allowed us to stuff the bears with a consistency better than hand stuffing. This also saved time and labor. These improvements helped the production of "made in the USA" Teddy Bears so that we could also expand the company into overseas manufacturing.

Our first ventures into overseas production of Winey Bear designs were for limited editions for customers. We were very pleased with the outcome of these products, and started to produce our own line of Bean and Bear products overseas. We eventually decided to work with other companies to produce Winey designs overseas. We currently have production through Cascade Toy on all plush lines and Planet Plush on all bean lines. In the past, we created designs for Annette Funicello, Sweet Memories, and several other companies.

Currently, Winey Bears provides the collector with a wide variety of choices from very inexpensive manufactured products to more costly one-of-a-kind handmade pieces. Along with all these products, I also design for private projects that do not carry my name as the designer. This full array of work makes Winey Bears a very fulfilling enterprise.

Winey Bears Studio in Morgantown, PA.

Sweet Baby Cheeks.

Mai Tai. My first manufactured Winey Bear. He is 4in (10cm).

CHAPTER 2

THE FIRST WINEY BEARS

Above: One of my first bears. He is made out of wool and has string eyes and nose, he is 10-1/2in (27 cm).

Above: This 17in (43cm) cotton weave patterned bear has it's arms and legs jointed and has plastic eyes and nose with leather paw pads and inner ears.

Susan is an 8-1/2in (22cm) curly wool bear. She also has her arms and legs jointed with miniature plastic eyes and nose.

Here is a limited edition bear.
He is number 15 of 50. It is a
16in (41cm), synthetic, fully
jointed bear with leather
paw pads.

Morton is a pellet filled,
German synthetic bear
with felt paw pads, glass
eyes, an embroidered
nose and mouth, and is
fully jointed. He is named
after our exchange
student, Morton,
from Denmark.

This unique bear was made
out of a blanket.

This fellow is a large bear with synthetic fur and short synthetic fur paw pads.

Sam is dressed up for the Forth of July, playing his role as Uncle Sam.

Jenny is waiting by the tree for her long awaited hug.

He is not ferocious;
nor is he scary. He
is the scarecrow
bear.

An antique looking
Santa Claus.

Earl was a unique design that I made. He has a hook neck and has jointed arms and legs, glass eyes, and embroidered nose and mouth.

Below: A compilation of bears and other creations that I made. They range from synthetic to mohair.

These wild creatures just love the outdoors. They love to play by the pond. They are all synthetic and handmade patterns.

Below: A Christmas compilation.

This bear can be found in Switzerland. He was hand dyed in coffee to give him an antiqued look.

These vintage style bears are decorated in antique ware. They are made of pink mohair with glass eyes and leather paw pads.

"Did anyone call for a cab?"
Here is the cab driver bear.
He is a 27in (69cm) mohair
bear.

Like all good bears he is taking his daily nap.

Winey the Who. This pattern is a unique pattern that I had designed and dressed in a plaid romper and hat.

A vintage style decorated bear in the *Winey the Who* pattern.

A mohair bear with leather paw pads, glass eyes, and embroidered nose and mouth.

A mohair bear for which I had designed the pattern. She is decorated in antique lace and a beautiful brooch.

Two of my first hand dyed items.

It's a girl! This limited edition of 10 is the perfect gift for newborn little girls.

The windowsill bear. She fits perfectly in any windowsill. She is made out of hand-dyed mohair and dressed in a handmade jumper.

All of the bears on these two pages are hand-died in the Winey Studios.

30

THE RAINBOW' COLLECTION

This is a 1992 bear with comprised of German synthetic fur with glass eyes and embroidered nose and mouth.

Johnny the Apple Seed bear. He was debuted at the apple festival in our little town.

Little Buddy is all ready for his sleepover with his pals.

CHAPTER 3

WINEY BEARS

Mix and *Match*
panda bears.

This family is made of German tipped mohair.

This Dream Catcher family is hand-dyed in anywhere from 3 to 12 different colors.

Bee and *Fuddles* are a cute pair. *Bee* is this little mohair bear with a sweater with a bee on it. *Fuddles* is the 3ft (.91M) string cotton bear.

All bundled up for
Christmas.

Earl is covered in
green tipped mohair
with paw pads hand-
died to match.

Snow Bear with his black hat and "coal" buttons is hoping summer doesn't come too soon.

Santa's Little Helper also became part of our collection.

This bear is all decked out for the holiday season in his red mohair suit.

Earl, with red curly mohair, and *Baby Earl* in green hand-dyed English mohair with red paw pads, are quite the pair.

THROUGH THE YEARS AT WINEY BEARS

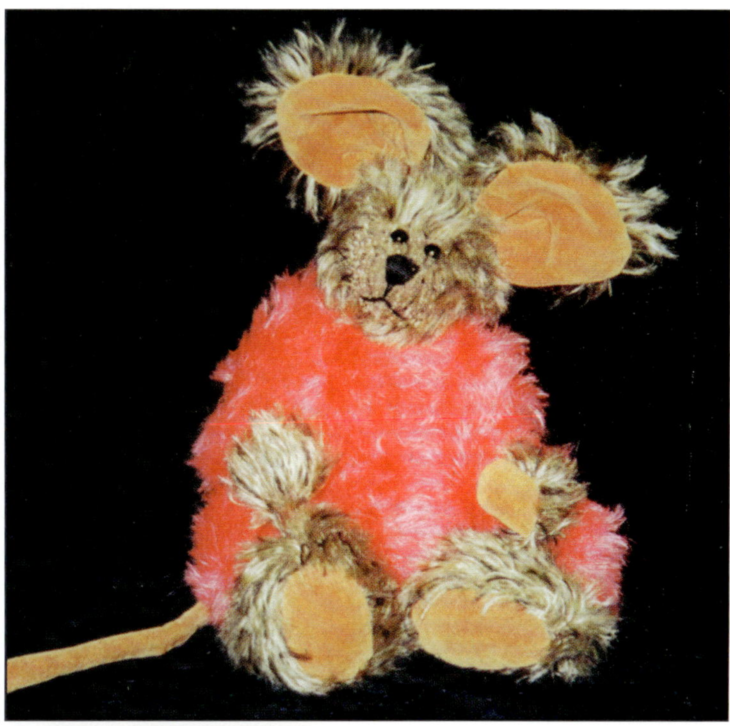

Top Left: *Ribbon Bear* is also in Christmas colors especially with his green embroidered nose.

Top Right: *Santa Mouse* wanted to come out and play too.

Christmas collections all hand spray painted to match the season.

Winey Originals

Hand-painted *Nick* pattern.

Sprayed all the colors of the rainbow.

Tipped *Earl*. Our unique pattern made of tipped mohair.

3ft (.91M) *Huey* is a hit in his many colors.

The colorful pattern on *Earl's* fur was painted on the material before it was cut out to make the bear.

FROM **A**ROUND THE **W**ORLD

MICHAEL MARECHAL'S GRANDPA BOPPY

Left and Below:
Grandpa Boppy

WINEY BEARS FROM GRUMBLE BEARS

Bear on all fours. It is a unique design and is made out of synthetic material.

Rosie the Cowbear.

Unique standing on all fours. Mohair dark brown with white tipped fur and light brown with white tip.

Velvet and silver ribbon bear.

Velvet ribbon bear.

Ribbon and wool bear.

GRUMBLE BEARS

Standing *F.A. Huey* in three different styles.

Simeon. A fun different style standing bear. Its head and arms are jointed.

Painted *Cuzzy Can't*.

A one-of-a-kind
long mohair bear.

A hand
sprayed
Kuzzy Kant.

Be Bears

This little hand-made mohair bear is cute and simple.

Sally Winey bear having fun.

FRANKEN WINEY FAMILY

Be Bears

Bears Will Be Bears

Bears can even be sprayed to suit the occasion like the two bears seen here. The BL Pattern bear seen above is all ready for Christmas.

The unique *Cuzzy Ken* rainbow bear. He is made out of hand-dyed fabrics and then is curled up into a ball because he can.

Hand-dyed green BL bear.

The hand-painted Mardi Gras colored bear.

A hand-dyed
German string
mohair *Berry* bear.

A pink tipped and
a pink dyed bear
having fun.

Part of the ribbon bear collection this
bear can never be duplicated it is a
one of a kind.

This fun bear is made
of red curly mohair.

This bear is covered in traditional curly mohair.

This brown mohair bear has curled legs that fit snug around you when you give him a little squeeze.

The *Mindy* bear, made of
pink mohair, is wearing a
knit dress my daughter
Mindy wore when she
was a little girl.

A prototype of *Earl*
made in 1999.
Remake of an
original made in
1989.

COLLECTING BEARS

I believe that every person collects bears for there own special reasons. I decided to ask bear collectors themselves why they collect teddy bears and which Winey Bear is their favorite. After reading why they collect teddy bears, ask yourself why you might collect a teddy bear. Then you have just found the best reason to become a collector.

QUOTES FROM BEAR COLLECTORS AND LOVERS

Why do you collect bears?

"I believe that teddy bears give unconditional love." - *Sally Winey*

"I collect all kinds of bears just simply because they remind me of my childhood years! And they are cuddly and comforting." - *Pat*

"I collect bears because no matter how hard or rough life can be or how sad and unhappy I may feel, the hug of a bear can make me smile and make the whole world seem a little brighter." - *Rick and Rhonda*

"I love Teddy Bears because they are always ready for a hug when I need one." - *Brian*

"The first toy that became my friend and constant bed partner that I dearly remember, was a musical teddy bear named Teddy. He was found in my bed when I woke up in the hospital after having my tonsils out at age 5. Teddy has been with me ever since. I think that formed my love for teddies." - *Pamela*

"How could you not love bears?!? They're so cute!" - *Amber*

"I have collected artist bears for several years now. I have always preferred teddy bears to dolls growing up. Teddy Bears always listen, are non-judgmental and are always in the mood for a hug! Sally Winey bears are a must to a bear collector! They have a personality-plus, are made with TLC and are so huggable. I have over 40 Winey Artist bears and continue to collect them because they "grab" me. I collect other artist bears as well, but Winey's come from the heart." - *Melissa from NC*

"Because my brother John, who is 10 years older then me, started giving me one for every birthday and Christmas since I was born; and I am 11 1/2 years old now." - *Alyson*

"Bears are adorable creatures!!! I love how they come in different colors, shapes, and sizes." - *Sarah*

"I collect bears because they are so cute and lovable and I go for the jointed bears the most" - *Dawn*

"I need that something special. I think that I like them because it is a transfer of affection for me. And bears make me feel good." - *Jean*

Neapolitan

Earl and *Sidney*

What is your favorite Winey Bear and why?

"I like *Earl* the best because he brings smiles to so many faces." - *Sally Winey*

"Oh, this is a toughy! I don't know if I can pick just one! One of my earlier favorites is *Cord-o-Roy*. Oh, and *Neapolitan*. One of my latest favorites is one that she made for me as a special order — a red, white and blue painted *Sidney*. The *Sidney* design is a favorite of mine too!!" - *Melissa from NC*

"My favorite Winey Bear is *Molly Blue* because I love the color blue and she reminds me of times past! She's beautiful." - *Pat*

"I love all of Sally's creations. I would have to choose *Sammy Claus* because he is my only real huggable size Winey Bear. Sally also signs him on the footpad. I actually spoke to her on the phone once about a set of her little bears. I was really impressed with her genuineness. She was so warm and friendly. This shows through in her beautiful bears." - *Rick and Rhonda*

"Probably have to say *Bamboodle* as he was my first and I love the black and white, Boston theme. Even more so, with Pandas so endangered it is simply wonderful to have one as a constant reminder of how precious nature is. My second favorite is *Walter Melon*. He reminds me of my husband Walt, whom I dearly love and who has been my partner for over 35 years." - *Pamela*

"My favorite Winey Bear is *Walter Melon*. He was the first Winey Bear that I bought and I just loved the innovative design and play on his name. His cute face got me hooked on Winey Bears forever." - *Brian*

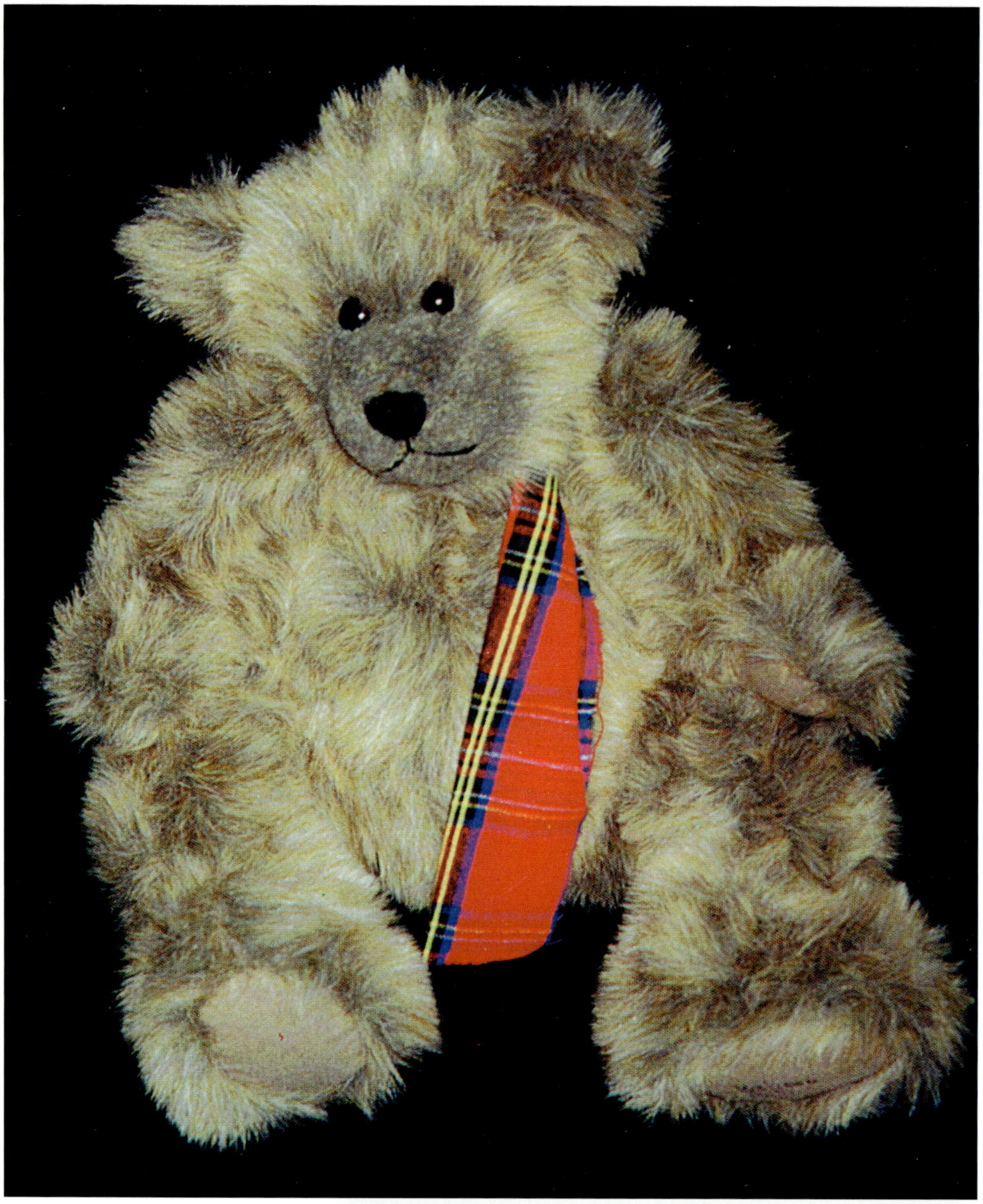

Sammy Claus

There are many reasons for bringing a new friend into your home. You may collect teddy bears because they remind you of your childhood, the unconditional love that they give, or just because you love teddy bears. Once you discover why you have became a bear collector, you have found the best reason for becoming one.

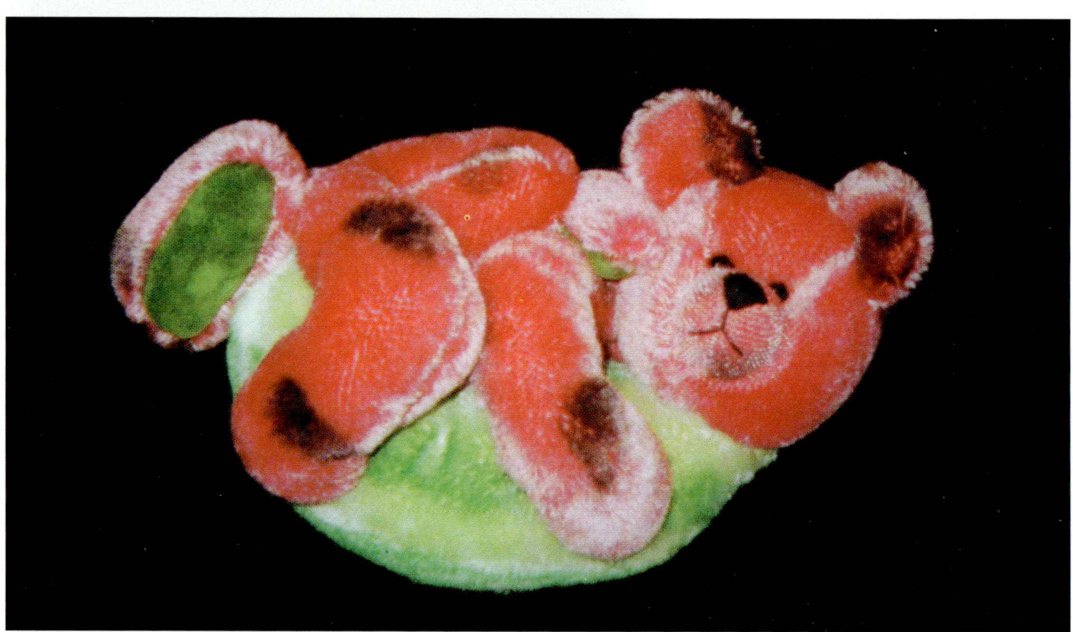

Walter Melon

CHAPTER 5

MATERIAL DECISIONS

There are many types of material to choose from. There are synthetics, which are man-made furs. They come in all different lengths, colors, patterns, and styles. Synthetic furs are usually less expensive to buy depending on where it is from and who makes it. You will be able to buy some synthetics at your local craft and fabric stores. For the more expensive and higher quality synthetics, look at the synthetics made in other countries or from companies that specialize in quality fabrics. The quality of the material affects the price of the bears. To check the quality of a synthetic material, you should notice whether it stretches, consider how thick the material is, and assess the intensity of the color. If the material is very stretchy, you will have to be careful not to overstuff your bear. Over stuffing will cause the bear to stretch and the bear's consistency can fluctuate. If the material is too thin, lines or patterns on the back of the fabric will show through. Thin material also makes the bear susceptible to holes and wear. Some of the synthetic materials will have rich deep colors and a pattern or design in the fabric. These materials make for some original and beautiful bears.

A *Sidney* made out of synthetic material.

Long Fellow made out of rose colored mohair.

Sidney, hand-painted white string mohair.

Mohair is the long, silky hair of the Angora goat. It is processed overseas in such places as England, Germany, and Africa. It is then shipped to the United States. This is why mohair is more expensive than synthetics. Mohair comes in a variety of lengths, colors, and textures. It can be long, short, or any lengths in between. Mohair can be wavy, curly, straight, puffy, soft, or stiff in texture, and tipped, solid, or spotted in color. If you can't find the exact color mohair that you would like, you can purchase white string mohair and dye the color yourself. If you want the string look, you should use German string mohair. If you want full, fuzzy, soft-colored mohair, you should purchase the English string mohair. The English string will "burst" during the dyeing process giving it the full look, while the German string will maintain the string look. Mohair is a high quality material. Any type of mohair will be more expensive than synthetic fabrics.

For a variety of fun and different styles and textures, there are many other materials to experiment with. Generally speaking, the price of the bear will depend on the price and quality of the material used. Silks are nice, but are a little harder to work with because of its smooth texture and it is lightweight. Silk bears are typically more expensive than synthetic bears due to the price of fabric and the time put into the creation. Tapestries are also a good fabric for making unique one-of-a-kind bears that can be priced accordingly. Wool can be good for making bears as well, but you should check the weave of the wool. If it is a loose weave, you may have problems with fraying and holes in the material while a tighter weave will make for a better bear. You can also use cottons or ordinary fabric for your bears. The prices of these bears are usually less than the price of synthetic bears. Bears made from cotton make nice lightweight bears that you can design to match a room, curtains, couches, or pillows. It's great for interior designing.

If you are making bears as toys for children, bears made from synthetics, cottons, and other ordinary fabrics are ideal. They are easy to manage, fix, clean. Also, they don't require any special attention and there is no worry of ruining a collectible. If you are making bears for collecting or designing, the higher quality fabrics are the best choice.

A bear made out of tapestry.

A tapestry bunny.

BRINGING COLOR TO YOUR BARE BEAR

What can you do when you have a great idea for a new teddy bear but you just can't find fabric the right color? There are a limited number of distributors who carry good quality material, and they can only sell the colors manufacturers choose to make. This presents a dilemma for bear artists and hobbyists. But there is a logical solution to this problem - create your own colors with dye!

There are basically two types of dye—natural and synthetic. Natural dyes are obtained from plants such as coffee, tea, indigo, saffron, red beets, and berries. Dying with natural materials can be messy and unpredictable, since you must steep your fabric in a bath of plant parts and water. However, the soft earth-tone colors produced by natural dyes are worth the fuss.

Synthetic dyes are derived from coal tar and are classified into 16 categories based on their chemical compositions and how they react to different materials. Most commercial dyes are synthetic. These dyes come in a range of colors, the intensity of which can be modified depending on the temperature of the dye bath and the length of time you leave the fabric in the solution (this is also true of natural dyes). The results from using a synthetic dye are more predictable than using natural dyes.

The color you seek and type of material you are dyeing will dictate the type of dye you choose. Some dyes work well on synthetic materials but not on mohair, alpaca, or wool. Check the labels on commercial dyes and synthetic materials to see if either specifically recommends compatible products for dyeing. In any case, dye a small sample of fabric before you immerse the whole piece in the bath. This allows you to check the effectiveness of the dye, its effect on the fabric, the intensity of the hue, and fabric shrinkage.

After you choose your fabric and dye, collect your tools. You'll need large pots and pans, a bucket or a bowl, spoons for measuring, rubber gloves to protect your hands, and an apron to protect your clothes. Depending on the dye you choose, the process may use hot water or cold water. Prepare your dying area in advance, so it's ready for your newly dyed fabric.

Follow the instructions on the dye package or in a book. In general, your dyeing process should involve pre-wetting the material then plunging it into a bath of dye solution. Stir the material constantly to assure the dye reaches all parts of the fabric. Be careful that you don't overcrowd the fabric in the container. If there is too much fabric in the dye pot,

Fill the washing machine with water and make sure that the dye is evenly stirred through out the water.

the dye cannot reach all parts of the fabric creating an uneven coloring of the material. Remember that the material in the dye bath will appear darker when wet than when it is dried. This is especially true of dark shades (black). 1 cup of vinegar for every 2-1/2 gallons of water helps. When you are satisfied with the color, remove the material from the dye and begin rinsing.

Sudden changes in temperature may "shock" certain materials such as mohair, alpaca, or wool. This shock damages the fibers in the material resulting in felting or matting. If this happens, the damage is irreversible. Do not bring the water to a boil. Remember to test a small (8-12 inches square) piece to check the fabric's reaction to hot water. Hot water will probably shrink your fabric - sometimes up to 30%. Measure carefully, allow for shrinkage, and dye enough fabric for your entire project at once. Make sure you take careful notes detailing your dye bath in case you need to make another batch. That way if you need more materials due to a mistake or because you miscalculated the color will be consistent.

Begin your rinse in hot water and gradually progress to warm, tepid, and finally cold water otherwise you will shock the fabric. Continue rinsing the

material until the water runs clear. This may take a while, but this assures your fabric will be colorfast. To remove the excess water from your material, place it in a muslin bag and spin dry it briefly in your washing machine. It is very important to remove the excess moisture from the material before you start drying it because overly wet fabric may drip and streak. Never dry your dyed fabric in direct sunlight, as this may have an adverse affect on the color or cause blotching. Never tumble dry wool or mohair because it will cause matting. Hang or lay the material in a dry, shady area. Do not hang the fabric directly on the clothesline; this may leave a line on the material. Pin the material to the line to avoid making marks as it dries.

After the fabric is dry, you may want to check it for colorfastness. There are four basic tests for fastness: washing, ironing, fading, and "crocking." Check for fastness against washing and ironing by washing a piece of dyed material in hot water then ironing it against a white cloth with a very hot iron. If it does not bleed, it is colorfast for both washing and pressing. Test for fastness against fading by leaving a piece of dyed material in direct sunlight for about 20 days. Finally, test for crocking, meaning that the color will not rub off against another material, by rubbing

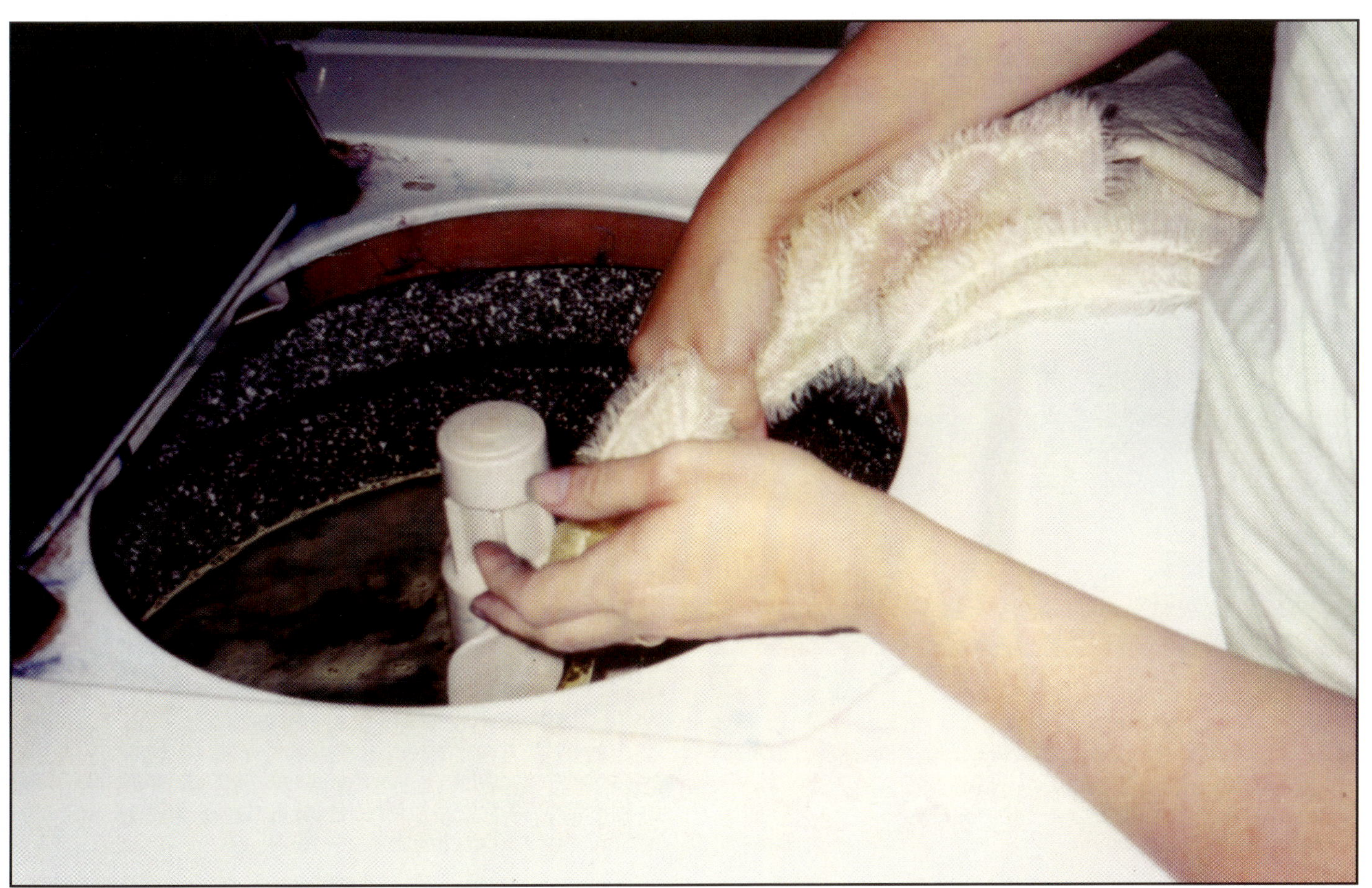

I am dyeing dream catcher material so I am putting spots on the fabric where I would like them to be.

both a wet sample and a dry sample against a piece of white cloth. If the color does not rub off, it is color-fast. If your fabric fails any of these tests, either avoid subjecting the finished bear to those conditions (e.g., washing), or repeat the rinse and dry cycles with the material. Using a mordant before dyeing may improve some material's color fastness. This is especially true for colors like black or red that are known for bleeding and fading. If you use a mordant, be sure to use non-reactive containers and utensils like glass, plastic, wood, or stainless steel. An alum mordant is the easiest and safest to use. You can make it by combining 4 oz. alum and 1 oz. cream of tarter in 2 cups of water. Put this mix into 4 gallons of water, and heat to 180°-200 F. After soaking the material for about an hour, let it cool to room temperature. You can then dye the material or let it dry for later.

Once you've mastered the basic dyeing process, the real fun begins—experimentation. Try mixing colors together; changing the water temperature (use a thermometer); modifying the length of time the fabric soaks in the bath (use a timer); wrapping the fabric with rubberbands for a tie-dye effect; or adding soap to felt or mat the pile. Use your own imagination to create your own unique techniques. Remember to test your ideas on a small piece of fabric before committing an expensive length of material to a radical new dye bath.

This is how I store the information on how I dye the material. I make sure to have a sample of what it looks like and all of the information that I need to know on how I made the material.

The most important part of a dye bath experiment and regular dyeing is taking notes. Write down everything you do and every factor in your process, from the water temperature to the soak time, and from proportion of dye to water to the drying location and time. This assures that you can reproduce a color that you love and avoid techniques that don't work out the way you imagined.

Dyeing your fabric is a great way to enhance the personal appeal of your bears and guarantee their originality. And, if there is only one shade for the teddy bear you dream of—try it!

This is one way that I dye fabric. You can also use a washing machine or any other non-reactive containers.

<u>Dye Record Sheet</u>

Capacity of dyebath container in gallons: _____ gallons

Total dry weight of material: _____ lb. _____ oz.

Dry weight of each batch to be dyed: _____ lb. _____ oz.

Type of material to be dyed: __________________________

Quantity of dye needed per batch: _____ lb. _____ oz.
_____ cups

Custom color formula: _____ yes _____ no

Formula: ______________________ Dye color _________ Amount

______________________ Dye color _________ Amount

______________________ Dye color _________ Amount

Cycle time ________ minutes   Temperature ________

Additives _____________________________________
(detergent, water conditioners, etc.)

Notes: ________________________________

____

____

____

____

Attach a color sample and/or product photo here

Dye Record Sheet

Capacity of dyebath container in gallons: _______ gallons

Total dry weight of material: _______ lb. _______ oz.

Dry weight of each batch to be dyed: _______ lb. _______ oz.

Type of material to be dyed: _______________________________

Quantity of dye needed per batch: _______ lb. _______ oz.

_______ cups

Custom color formula: _______ yes _______ no

Formula: ______________________ Dye color ____________ Amount

______________________ Dye color ____________ Amount

______________________ Dye color ____________ Amount

Cycle time ____________ minutes   Temperature ____________

Additives ____
(detergent, water conditioners, etc.)

Notes:______________________________________

____

____

____

____

Attach a color sample and/or product photo here

HAND-PAINTED BEARS

I love spray-painting bears. I feel like this is a true form of bear artistry because you actually create the bear and then paint it as if you are creating a masterpiece of the truest art form.

Supplies needed:

1. Rubber Gloves — *should be worn when working with spray.*

2. Face mask — *to protect yourself from the fumes.*

3. Paper towels — *to wipe up excess spray runs and to get the paint off of the bear's eyes.*

4. Air Brush & Paint or Flora Spray Paint — *flora spray paint can be found at your local craft store.*

5. Material — *chose the type of material you would like.*

6. Dog or Teddy Bear Brush — *to brush out the material/bear when the paint is dry. This will bring the softness back.*

7. You will either need a spray paint booth or spray outside — *make sure that there is plenty of ventilation so the fumes will be pulled away.*

8. Read all of the directions and cautions on the paint can for your safety.

There are a couple different ways to create a spray-painted bear. The first way is to paint the material before drawing on and cutting out the pattern. The second is to paint the bear after it is already made.

When I paint the material first, I hang the material outside using a piece of plywood to support it and then paint the material before I put the bear together. You can create unique designs, murals, or whatever you want to do. Then you can lay your pattern pieces in different ways to get the effect you are looking for.

When painting the finished product, I make the bear first and then airbrush the bear. It is a good idea to practice on a test bear before you make the final version. Think about what colors will look good together and which ones will clash. You can get a color wheel at your local art store that will help with color combinations. When you paint your bear, make sure you cover the whole bear paying special attention to the areas under the arms and in-between the legs. Be careful to hold the can far enough away from the bear so that you don't over paint an area.

You can also paint the fabric with fabric markers. This allows you to create even more unique designs. Please try different types of markers and dyes to get your own special effects.

Read the label on the paint can for directions on how to wash the material that you have painted. You can also check how it reacts by testing a small piece of material. Please follow the instructions on the can for the safety cautions of the paints you are using.

To store your painted bear, keep it out of direct sunlight and out of damp areas.

There are many colors to chose from.

Spraying a bear to tip its fur coral.

Finish up the front making sure that under the arms and between the legs are sprayed.

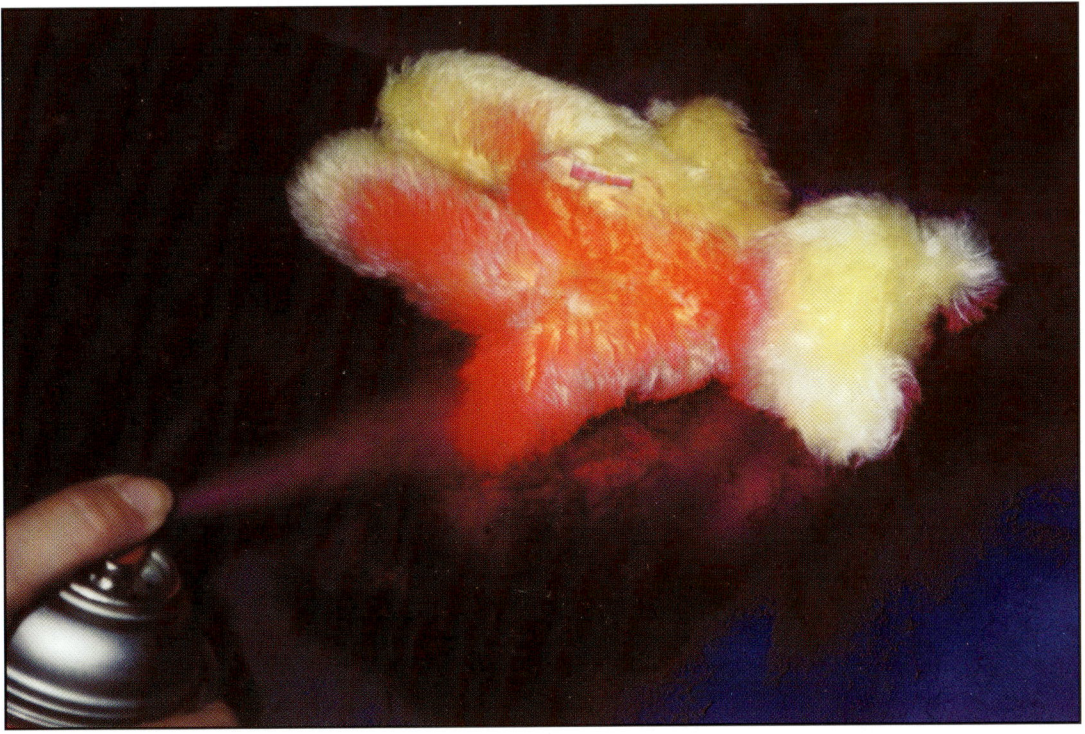

Then do the back of the bear.

This will soon be flash fire rainbow bear. You will want to make sure that you have red, orange, yellow, green, blue, and purple.

Start with red at the top of the head. This can be started with any color but if you want it rainbow be sure to follow ROY G BIV.

Then spray orange so that there is no white between the red and the orange. Make sure to go around the whole bear when painting.

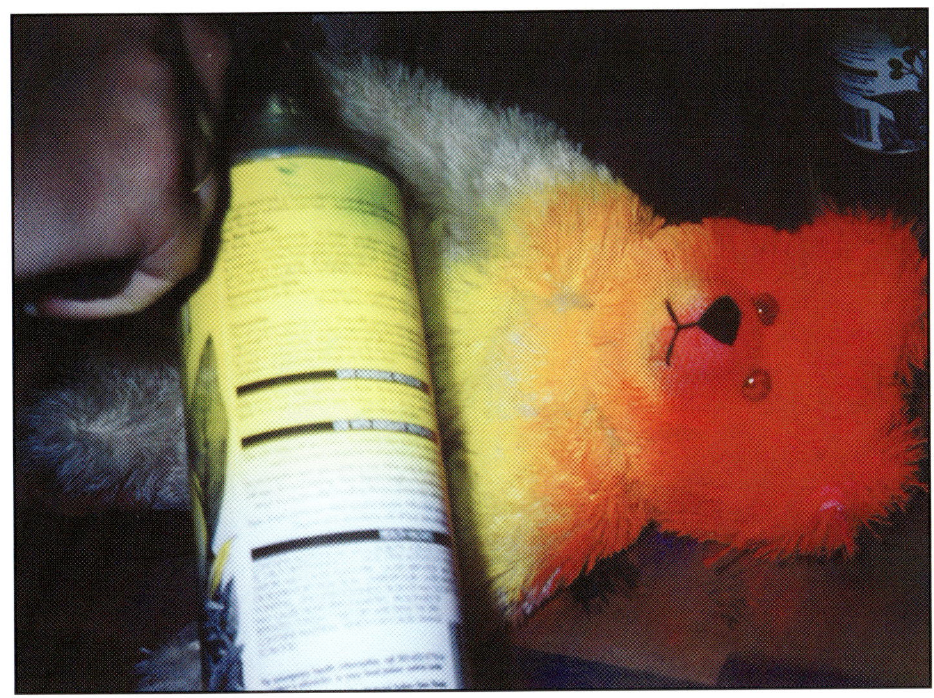

Then the yellow comes next.

Then spray all of the green around under the yellow.

Then the blue. You will want to make sure that you get under the arms and between the legs. No white should be showing. If there is white showing color the material according to the color it is next to.

Finally, the purple.

After the touch up paint, wipe the paint off of the eyes, and let the bear dry. After he is dry, you will want to brush his fur to make it fluffy.

SUPPLIES

The Tools Needed

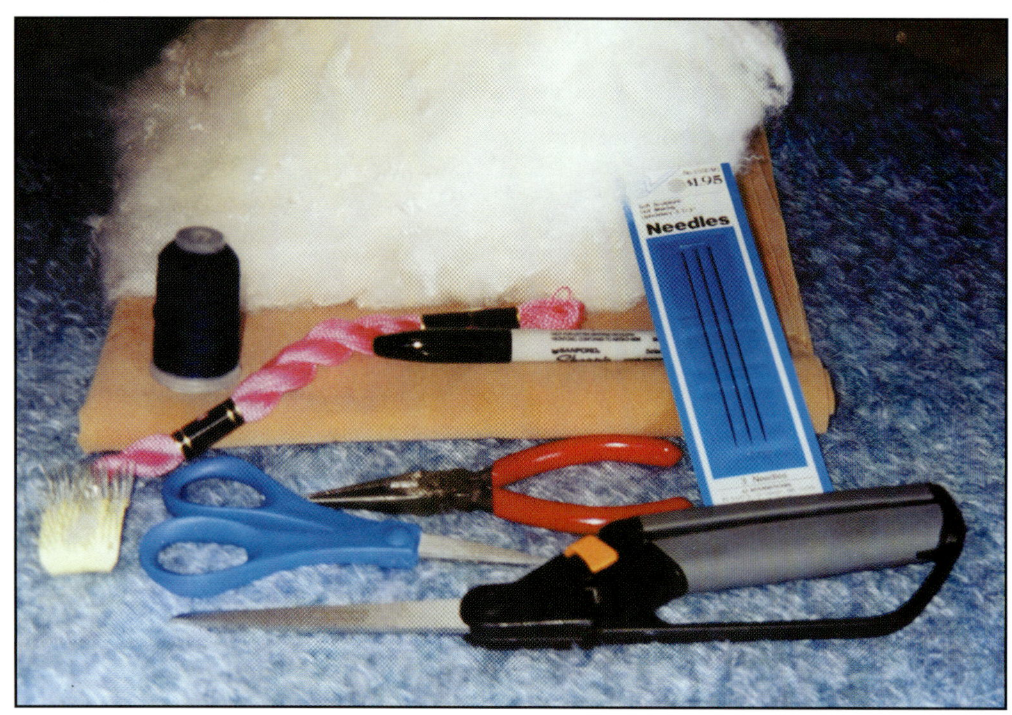

Before starting your project, make sure that you have all of the necessary supplies. This makes the project easier and faster. You can buy the supplies at your local craft store, hardware store, or from the specialty stores that sell bear-making supplies (look at the Resources section at the end of this book for these stores.) If you are unable to find an item, a similar tool can be substituted.

These are the supplies needed for making the bear in the order that you will use them.

1. **Material**
   If you are dyeing the material, you will need:
   a. Rubber gloves
   b. A dyeing pan or washing machine
   c. Choice color of Rit dye
   d. Stirring stick

2. **Pattern**
   Make sure that it is not the original and that it is on a piece of poster board or thicker piece of paper.

3. **Fine Point Permanent Marker**
   Watch that the marker does not show through the material. If it does, make sure that you do not to make any unnecessary marks on the material.

4. **Scissors**
   A pair of sharp scissors and a pair of smaller sharp scissors are suggested. You can just buy a pair of small sharp scissors if desired. The larger scissors are used for cutting out the fabric while the smaller pair is suggested for cutting the thread.

5. **Quilting Pins**
   Choose larger pins with the balls on the ends so that no pins get lost in the bear.

6. **Sewing Machine**
   It is easier to sew the bear on a machine then by hand unless you are making miniature bears.

7. **Thread**
   Choose thread that matches the material you chose for your bear. You can use regular sewing machine thread for the machine sewing of the bear.

8. **Stuffing Stick**
   This can be anything that is strong (usually made out of wood) and is about 8"-12" (20cm-31cm) in length. It should be cylindrical and about the same diameter as the marker. This helps with the turning of the bear and the stuffing of the bear. It helps ensure that the paw pads are stuffed firmly so there are no gaps in the fabric.

9. **Stuffing**
   Poly-fil works great. You can get it at any local craft store.

10. Plastic Joints or Wooden Disks and Cotter Pins

Plastic joints can be found in either your local craft store or specialty bear-making stores. Wooden disks and cotter pins can be found in the hardware store or in a craft store. Make sure that you have the correct size joints for the bear. If the pieces are too small, they will make the joints seem loose. If they are too large, the pieces will not fit.

11. Doll Making Needles

Use these to sew the joints in place and to sew up the back.

12. Strong Carpet Thread

When sewing joints in place, you need a stronger thread that will not break when you pull it. This ensures that the bear's arms, legs, and head will not come off when they are twisted. You will also use this thread for the eyes.

13. Awl

This is used to make holes for the eyes so that the fabric will not tear. If you cannot use an awl, us the tip of the small scissors.

14. Large Doll Making Sculpting Needle

You will use it to put the eyes on your bear. It must be long enough to go through the front of the head to the lower back of the head so that the eyes remain secure.

15. Eyes

You need either plastic or glass eyes. Some plastic eyes need to be put in place before you stuff the head. Be aware of the kind of eyes that you buy. Eyes come in all different shapes, sizes, and colors. Choose the kind of eyes that appeal to you the most.

16. Nose Floss

Pearl Cotton is preferred for the nose, but if you are unable to use it, you can use embroidery floss. There are also plastic noses that you can put on before the stuffing of the head.

17. Pliers

Pliers are helpful when a needle is too difficult to pull through the fabric. They can easily grip the needle and help pull the needle through.

18. Dog or Bear Brush

There are dog and bear brushes that have fine pin-like bristles that help pull the bear's fur out of the seams and fluff the fur. Be careful with some materials. This brush can rip the fur out or it can make the fur's consistency (wavy to fluffy or stringy to fluffy). If you use a special fur that cannot be brushed out, use a needle to pull the fur out of the seam.

19. Ribbon

Choose a ribbon that most suits your bear. Make sure that you have enough ribbon.

CHAPTER 9

MAKING YOUR BEAR

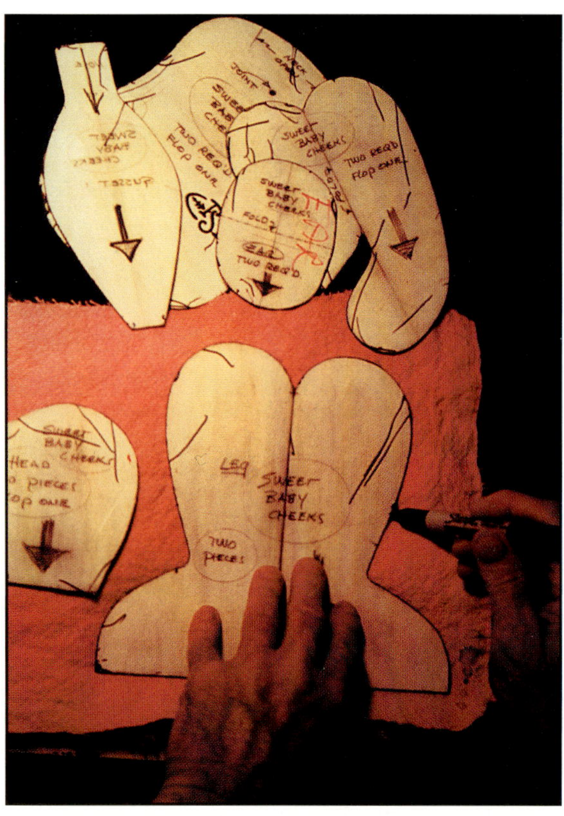

Drawing the pattern
onto the material.

Step 1
Transferring the Pattern

Pick the desired pattern. Then, using a piece of plain white paper, tracing paper, or wax paper, trace the pattern pieces onto the paper keeping the original in a file in case of loss or damage to the pattern pieces. Take note to place all of the dots, arrows, lines, and words onto the new pattern. You may want to transfer the pattern onto a thicker board such as card stock, poster board, or cardboard especially if you are planning to make more than one bear. Make sure that when you cut out your pieces that you always cut on the inside of the line. After you have all of your pieces traced on, cut out, and labeled the same as the original, you can go to the next step.

Step 2
Preparing the Material

First, make sure that you have enough material for the bear you are making. For the *Sweet Baby Cheeks*©1998, for *Some Bear from Over the Rainbow*©1998, and for *Baby Flash Fire*©1998 you will need 1/4-yard (23m) of material. This will help ensure room for mistakes or extra bears. Preparation and drawing on for *Some Bear Over the Rainbow*©1998 is in step 3b. Make sure that you allow 4.5" X 11.5" (12cm X 29cm) of material for the paw and footpads.

Next, check the nap (see diagram 1). The nap is the way the fur lays. For example, when you rub your hand on the material, does the fur lie flat and smooth or does it stand up and give more resistance. For your bear to be smooth and nice-looking, the nap should always go down. In that case, place the material with the nap going downward towards you.

Step 3
Drawing the Pattern on the Material

For *Sweet Baby Cheeks*©1998 and *Baby Flash Fire*©1998, place the patterns on the material with the arrows pointing down (the arrows signifie which way the nap should go for that piece). Then trace the patterns onto the fabric. A permanent marker can be used to trace the patterns onto the material. Do not write the directions or put the arrows on the fabric. The marker can bleed through some fabrics and the extra writing can ruin the bear. If a pattern says to cut 2, you need to draw the one side then flip the pattern over and draw its other side. It should be a mirrored image of the first. Finally, draw on the paw and footpads using the material you have chosen. Draw one of each and then flip the pattern over and draw its other side.

Step 3b
Preparing and Drawing on for a Rainbow Bear

A rainbow bear takes more than one color of material. You need about 5 different colors. You can either buy 5 different materials or you can buy one kind of material and cut and dye it yourself. Look back at chapter 6 for directions on how to dye material. For example, I suggest that the arm is not the same color as the side of the head, body, or leg. You can do a symmetrical color scheme so that the body is blue, the head is red, both arms are yellow, both legs are green, and both ears are orange for example. Or you can do an asymmetrical color scheme by randomly matching the colors. You can also do themes of favorite colors, countries, or schools. After choosing your color scheme, go back and look at steps 2-3 to learn about the nap and the way to draw on the bear.

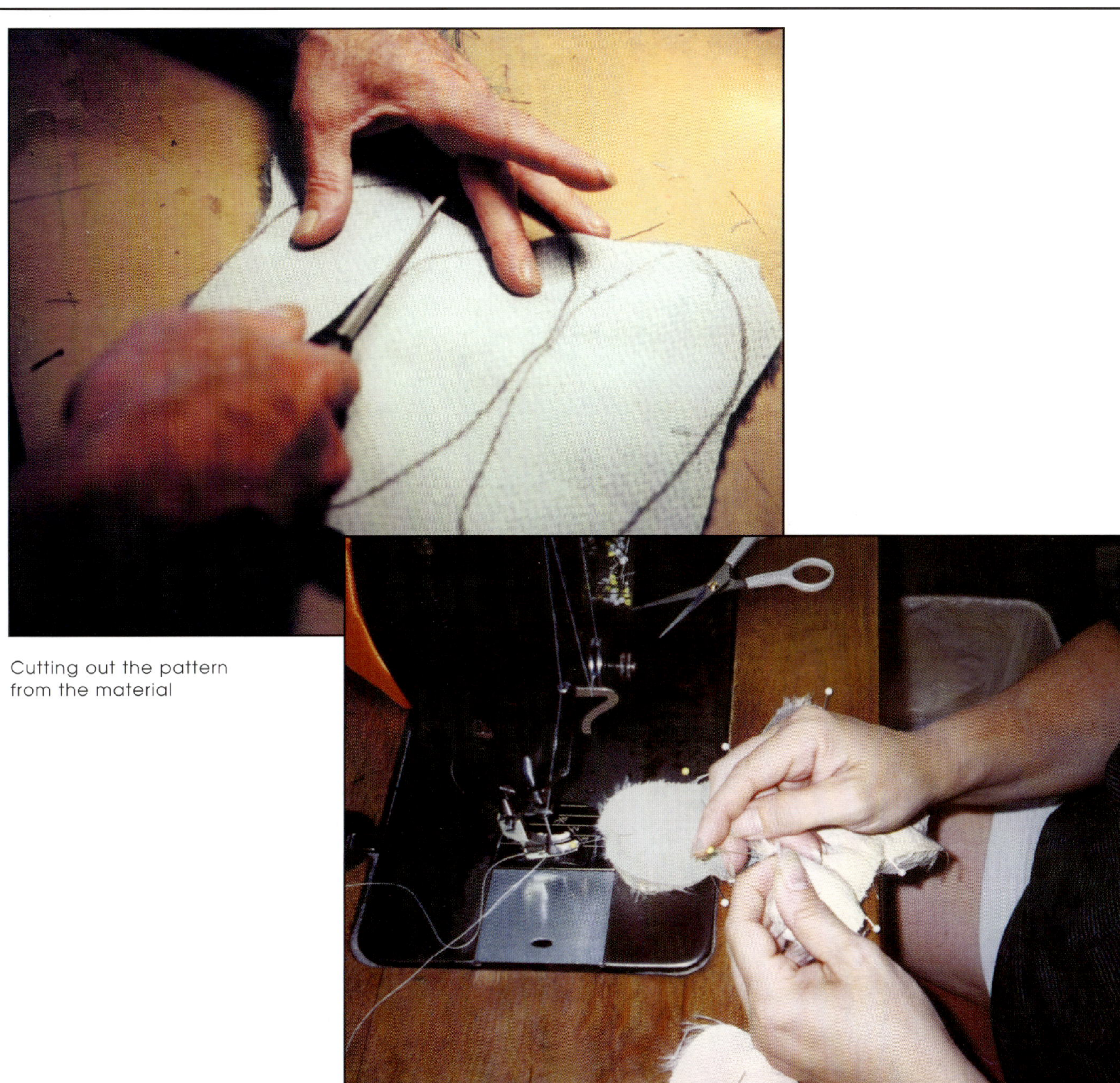

Cutting out the pattern from the material

Pinning the pieces together.

Step 4
Cutting Out Your Bear

You will need a sharp pair of scissors so that you do not fray or chew the fabric. To cut out the bear you must cut on the black line of the pattern pieces, take small cuts with the scissors close to the back of the fabric to ensure that you don't accidentally cut the length of the fur. Then, cut out the paw and foot pads. After all of the pieces are cut out, you will be ready to go to step five.

Step 5
Pinning Your Bear

First, lay out all of your pieces. Then, group the pieces together—the two sides of the bodies go together, the two sides of the heads and the gusset, the arms and the paw pads, legs and foot pads, and the ears. Next, pin the pieces together. Put the sides of the material that you want to show facing together so that the backside of the material is what you see. Use large quilting pins to pin the pieces together. The last thing you want to do is lose small pins in the bear's fabric. Ouch!

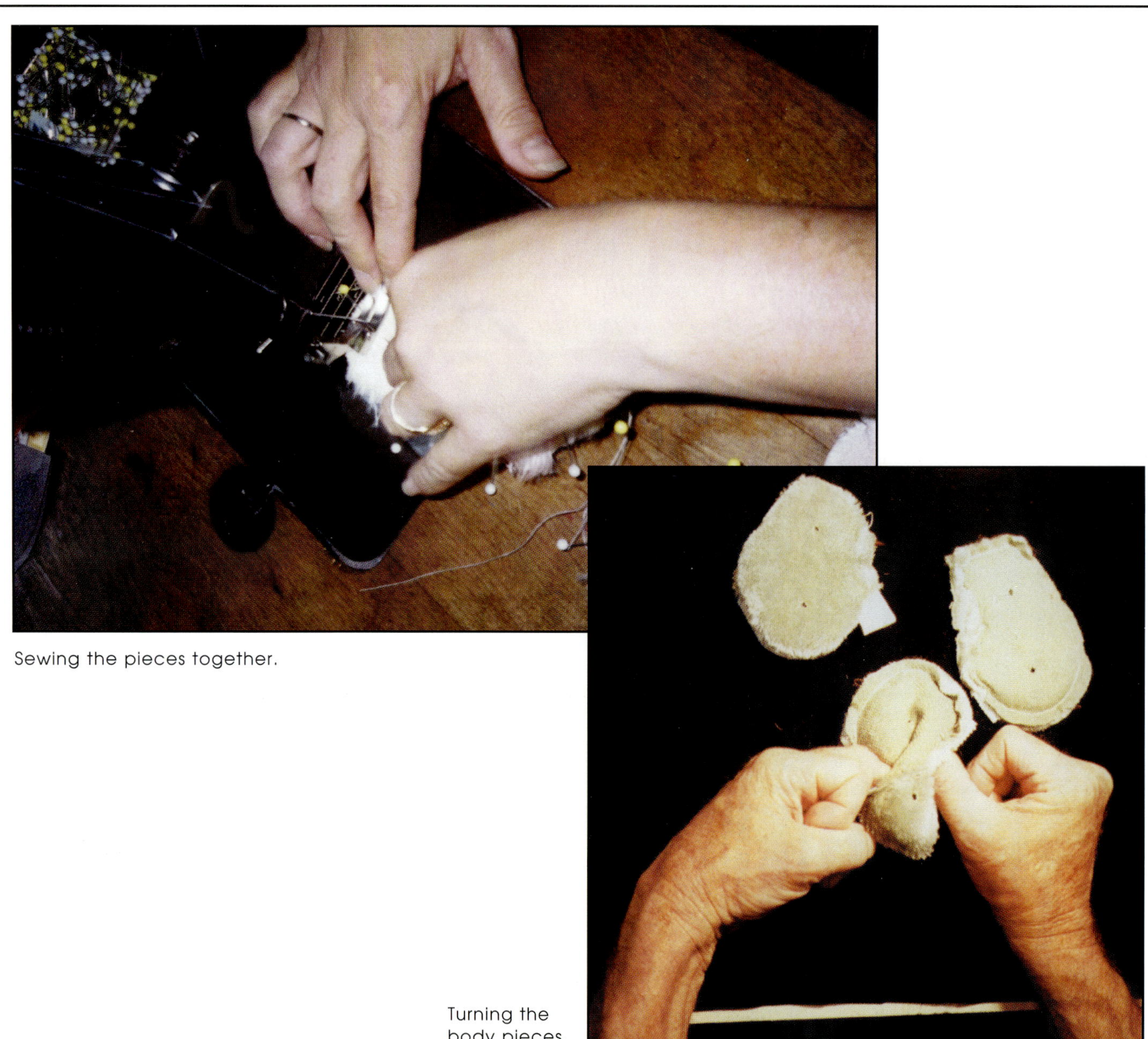

Sewing the pieces together.

Turning the
body pieces.

HEAD:

There are three pieces to the head—the gusset (#1) or the center of the bear's head, the right side of the head (#2), and the left side of the head (#2). Pin and sew a 1/4" (65cm) seam on both the right and left sides of the head from point *A* to point *B*. This is the chin seam (see diagram 1). Then insert the gusset (#1). Pin point *A* on the sides of the head to point *A* on the gusset and then sew the gusset into the head (see diagram 2). You should leave an opening at the bottom of the neck to turn the head. A trick to turning is to start at the furthest part of the head (the nose) and push it through the opening. Set the head aside until you are ready to stuff the bear.

EARS: (#7)

Fold the ear piece in half and sew from point *G* to point *H*. After it is sewn, cut a slit long enough to turn the ear on the fold of ear. Be sure to keep the edges clean.

BODY: (#8)

If there are darts in the body, sew them up. These will help give roundness to the body. However, some patterns do not have darts, which is fine. It depends on the way each bear looks. After any darts are sewn up, put the two sides of the body together. Pin them and sew them from points *I* to *J* (see diagram 3). Make sure to leave an opening in the neck if the pattern requires. Leave a hole in the back of all bear bodies for turning and stuffing.

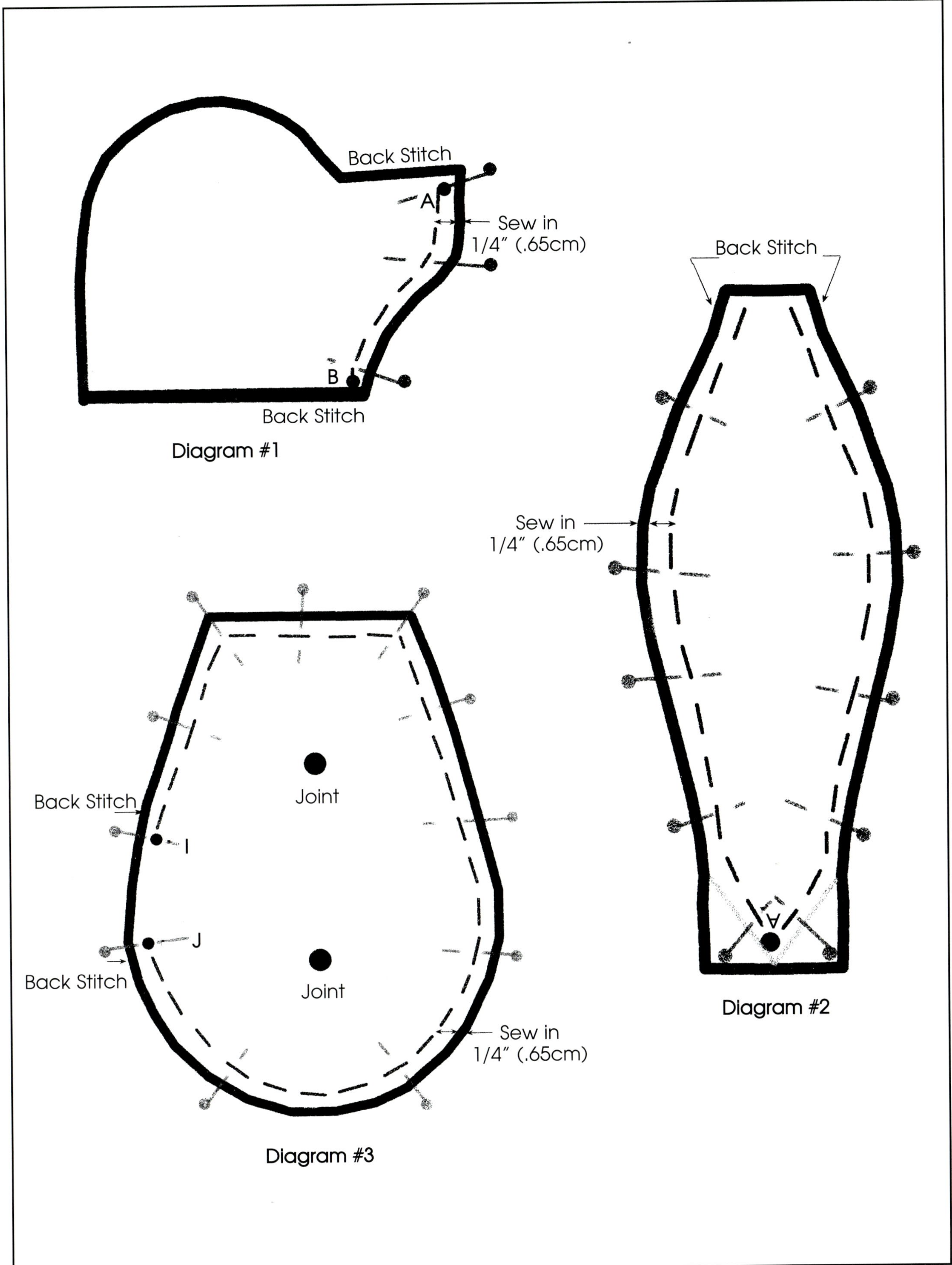

Back Stitch
A
Sew in
1/4" (.65cm)
B
Back Stitch
Diagram #1
Back Stitch
Sew in
1/4" (.65cm)
A
Diagram #2
Joint
Back Stitch
I
Joint
J
Back Stitch
Sew in
1/4" (.65cm)
Diagram #3

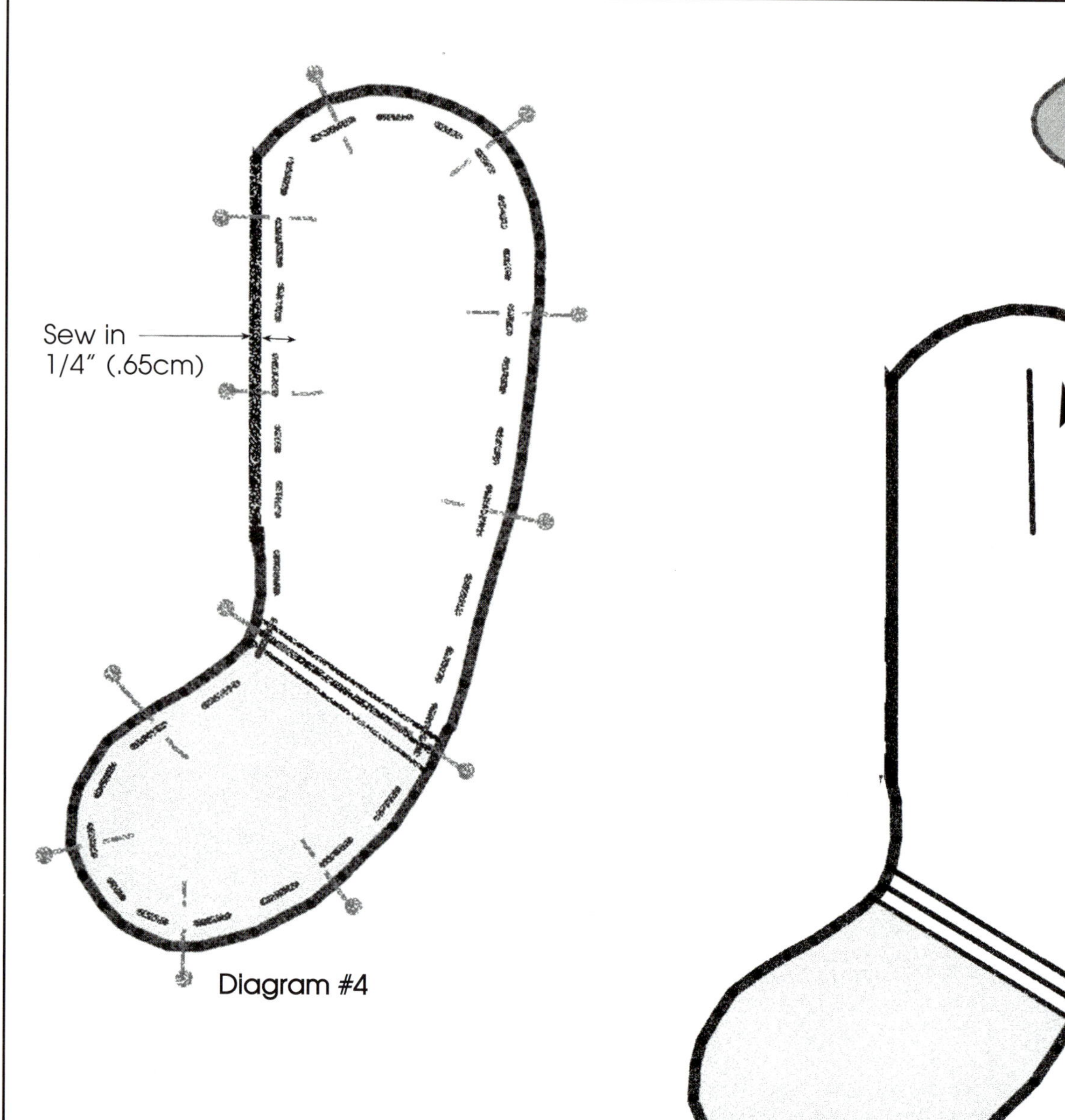

ARMS:

First, sew the paw pad (#3) to the inner arm (#4) by matching up points *C* and *D*. Fold the arm piece and sew around the bear's arm, making sure not to sew over the folded area. Leave no openings (see diagram 4). If your bear has a two-piece arm, sew on the paw pad and then pin both pieces together. Sew completely around the arm with no opening. Then, on the inside of the arm, centered in the shoulder part, cut an opening large enough for the joint to fit through (see diagram 5). Turn the arm through the hole from the tip of the paw. Set aside for stuffing.

LEGS:

Fold the Leg (#5) in half on the line. Sew the leg from the top of the toe (*E*) to the top of the fold (see diagram 6). There is no need to sew along the fold. Leave the bottom of foot open. Then pin the footpad (#6) into the opening, centering points *E* and *F* (see diagram 7). You can baste the footpad in place for easier handling. If you do not have a back seam in the *F* point, make a very small clip in the material so that sole of the foot fits better. When you are finished sewing the leg, make a cut in the center part of the inner legs where the joint is to be placed for turning. Again, turn the pieces and set aside for stuffing (see diagram 8).

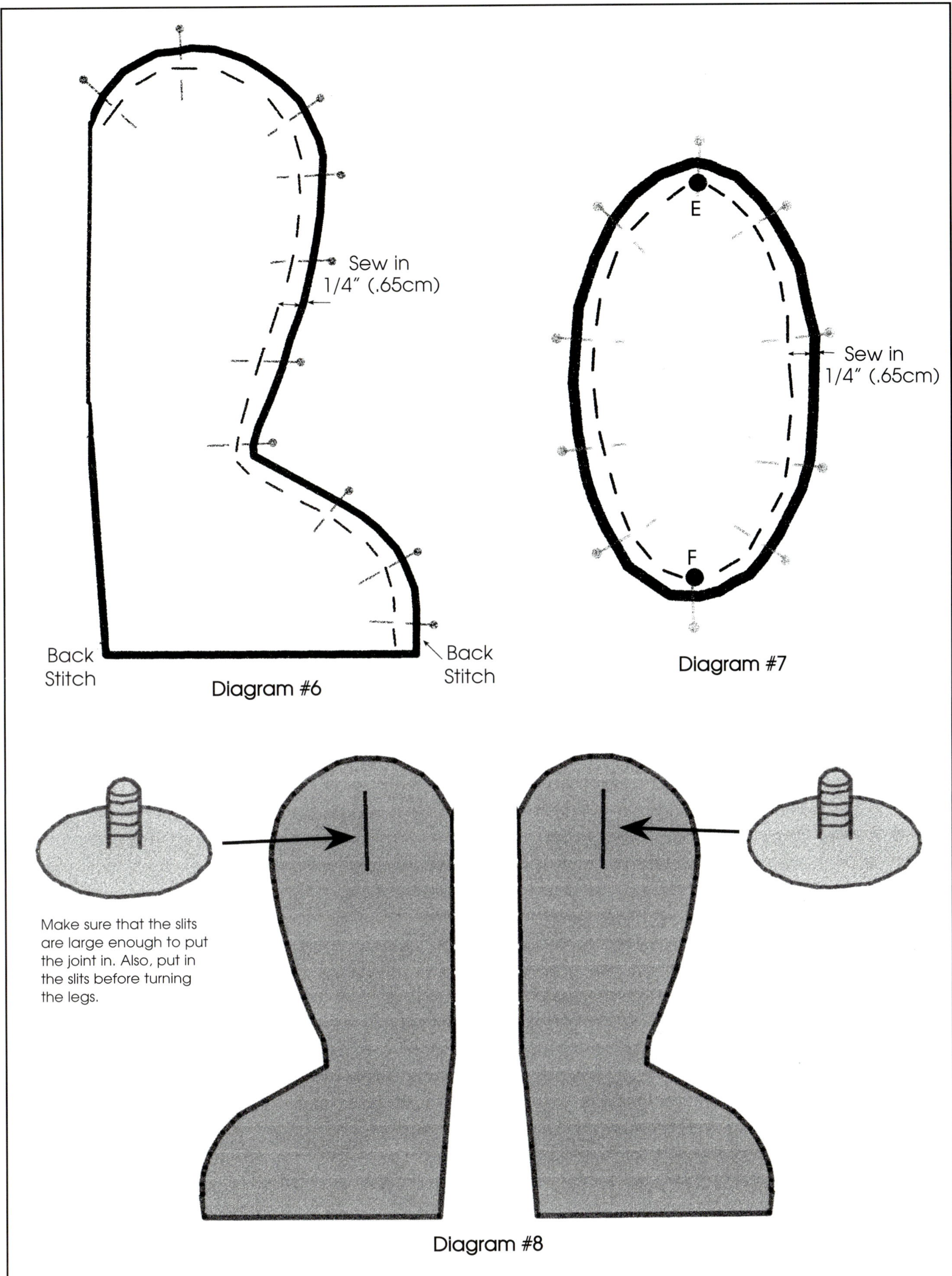

Sew in 1/4" (.65cm)
Back Stitch
Back Stitch
Diagram #6
E
Sew in 1/4" (.65cm)
F
Diagram #7
Make sure that the slits are large enough to put the joint in. Also, put in the slits before turning the legs.
Diagram #8

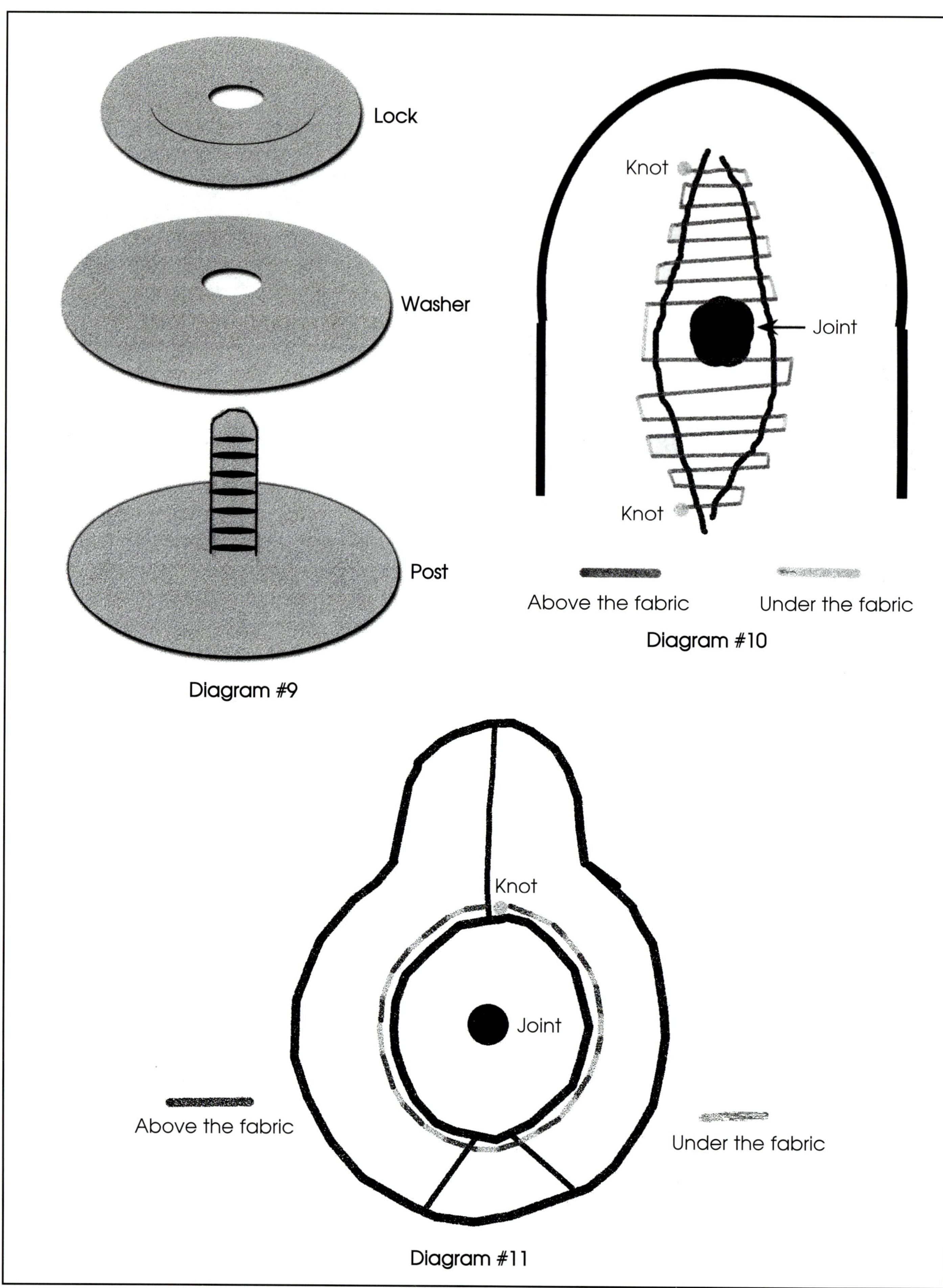

Diagram #9

Diagram #10

Diagram #11

Make sure all of the parts are turned completely paying special attention to the nose. Start by stuffing the head firmly. The firmer the nose is, the easier it is to sew on the nose. As you practice, you will get a feel for sculpting your bear's head and how to fill it to create your own special look. Many people do not realize the importance of this step. Material stretches and should be equally stuffed on each side of the head. You can make the arms and legs firm or soft and you can use either pellets or stuffing. It's up to you. Just be consistent with whatever you choose. The stuffing should fill the arms and legs all the way to the top. The joint will then be placed on top of the stuffing.

There are many different types of jointing styles. Some people use cotter pins, or buttons, others use nuts and bolts. I have found that plastic doll joints work very well in the smaller bears. To determine the size you need for your bear, you need to measure the size of the arm and leg area. The common sizes are as follows.

Sweet Baby Cheeks©1998
 Head - 45mm. Arms - 35mm. Legs - 45mm.
Baby Flash Fire©1998
 Head - 30mm. Arms - 20mm. Legs - 20mm.
Rainbow Bear©1998
 Head - 35mm. Arms - 30mm. Legs - 35mm.

There are three parts to a joint: a post, a washer, and a lock (see diagram 9). Now, place the posts in the head, arms, and legs. For the arms and legs, sew in place by using a ladder stitch (see diagram 10). For the head, use a gathering stitch around the opening and pull it tight around the post knotting it tightly (see diagram 11). Then sink the knot by bringing the needle out at a different place in the appendage. This leaves a "tail" inside the piece so the knot will not unravel or untie. You should always sink the threads back into the appendage any time you make a knot.

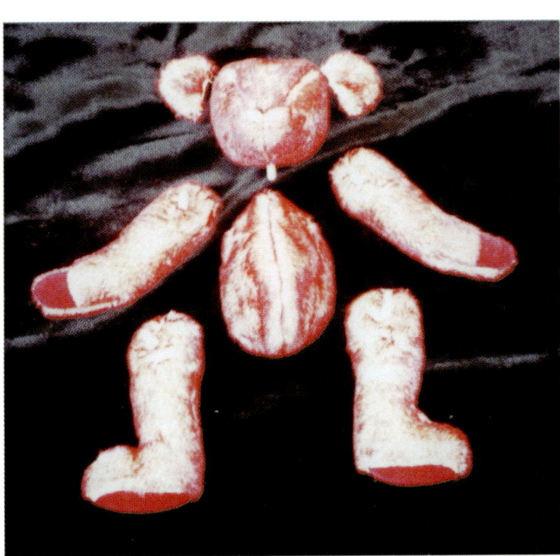

How to place the pieces. Put on the head first, then the arms, and finally the legs.

Be certain that you have the small holes cut in the body for the arms and legs before you turn the body. Turn the body. Now attach the limbs as seen in the illustration at left. Start with the head. Make sure that the head hole is centered, on the top of the body, and a little off center of the seam either to the right or left. If you cut through the seam, it will unravel the rest of the seam.

After placing the posts through the body, place the washer on top of the post inside the body, and place the lock on top of the washer with the flat side down. Then press down on the lock as far as it will go. My secret to making sure they are locked tightly is that I get my husband to help. Finally, stuff the body to the preferred and use the ladder stitch to close the back. No threads should be seen.

You might look at your little guy and not want to shave his face, but if you do decide to shave it, now is the time to give him a trim. No matter what, you must trim away the fur from the nose area to help sew the nose on.

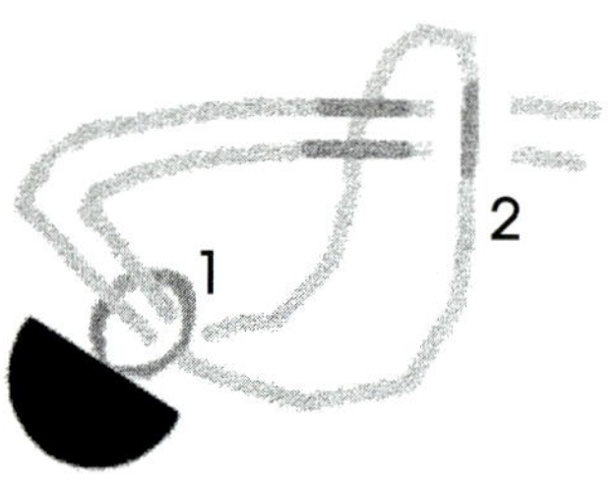

1) Cut one long string then fold it in half. Take the end with the two open ends and stick it through the back of the eyehole.
2) Stick the two open ends through the loop of the other end of he string.
3) Pull tight.

Diagram #12

1) Place eyehole where you want them. Then place the eyes in the holes and pull the needle to the back of the head shown at #2.
2) Bring both of the strings out this hole. Knot the threads and hide the knot.

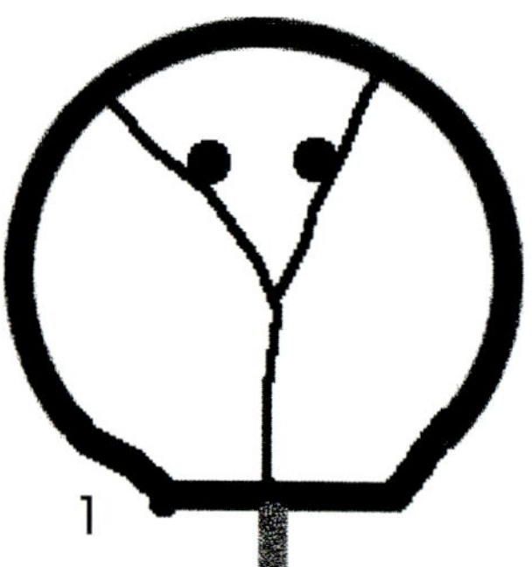

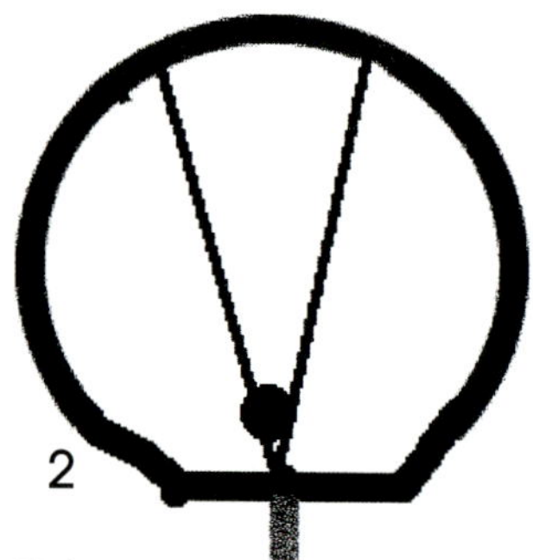

Diagram #13

EYES

String strong thread through the back loops of the eyes (see diagram 12). The placement of the eyes is up to you. They should be either on the outside or inside of the gusset seams—not on the seams. Use your awl to poke a hole in the fabric for one of the eyes and pull the threads out the back lower part of the head. Set the first eye into the head. Use the placement of the first eye to guide you in placing the second eye. This is better than marking the placement with dots. Insert the second eye and come out the back lower part of the head about 1/4" (.65cm) away from where the first eye came out. Tie off the threads several times while pulling tightly on the threads. Finish by sinking the knot back into the head (see diagram 13).

Stringing the eyes.

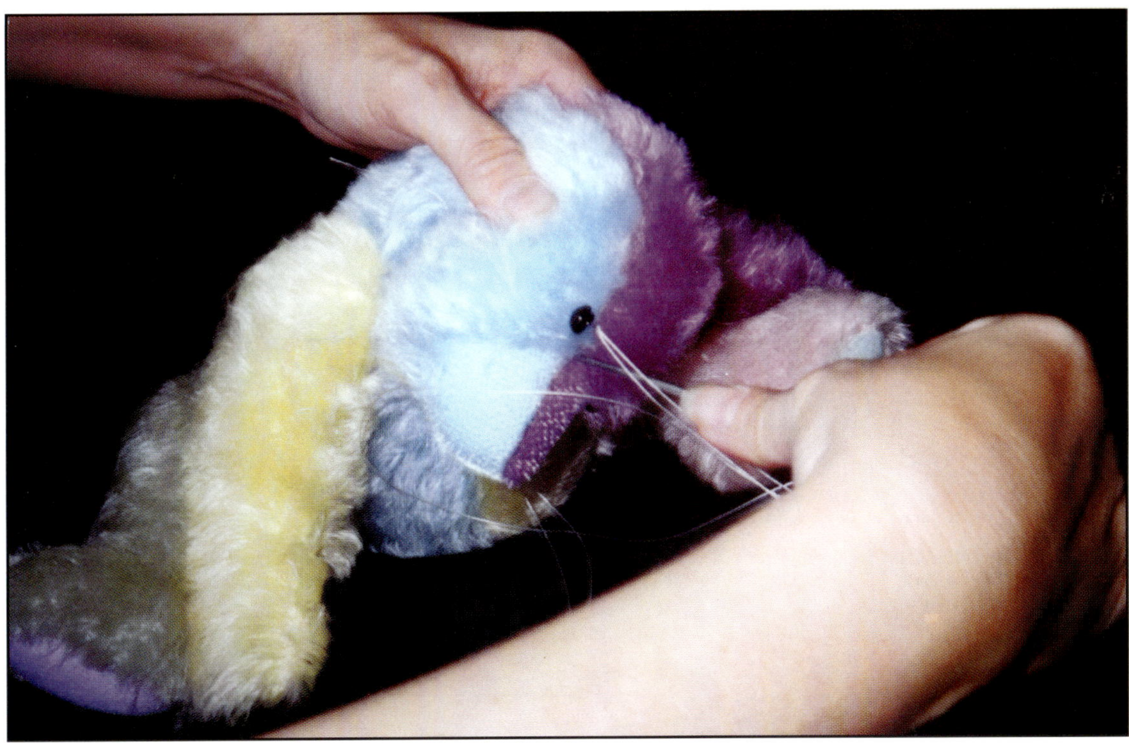

Putting the eye in place.

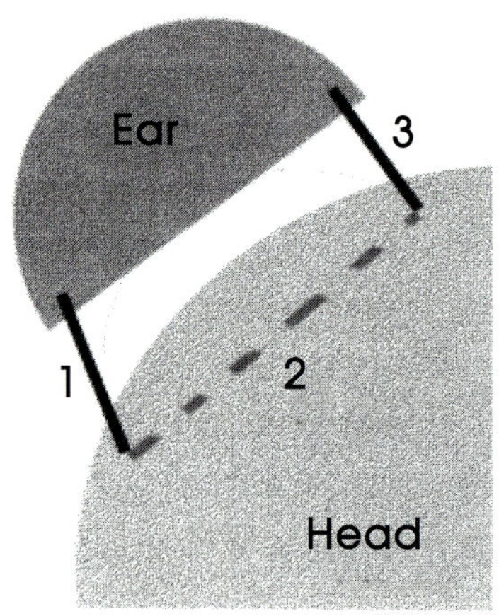

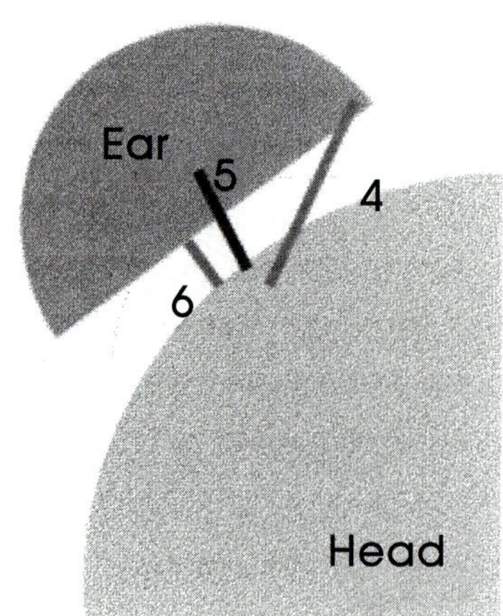

1) Start with the thread knotted and have the knot in the ear.
2) Put the needle into the head where you want the ear to start and pull out the needle where you want the ear to end.
3) Put the needle in the ear and pull it out.
4) Then place the needle into the bear's head where you had just pulled it out of and bring it out in the center and back a little from the line of the ear.
5) Grab the front of the ear and put the needle through the front to the back and place the needle back into where the thread is coming out of.
6) Pull tight. Then make sure that you tack the rest of the ear down so there is no raw edges showing.

Diagram #14

With embroidery stitching either back and forth or up and down place the nose on the bear. Do not knot off the thread, clip off the end.

Diagram #15

EARS

I do not put any stuffing in the ears, but you can if you want. I use a unique method that makes placement easier. You don't need to pin or mark your bear. Take your needle through the top edge of the ear that is being placed (see diagram 14). Then enter the needle in the location on the head where you want the ear, and pull the ear to the head and see if you like the location. When you find the proper look for your bear, bring the needle out at the bottom of the area you want the ear to stop. Insert the needle a little below this point and pull it out in the center of the ear a little back from center line. This creates a tuck in the ear. Come back through the ear and knot. Now, sew a few more stitches to turn raw edges under and add strength to the ear. Tie off and sink the threads into the head. Repeat for the other ear matching it with the first.

NOSE

This is the fun part. Be creative. Look around at other bears and decide what you like the best. I am going to share with you my method of sewing on noses. First, I make an outline and then fill it in. Look at the illustration for guidance (see diagram 15). Last but not least, stitch the smile.

Step 11
Finishing the Bear

To finish your bear, brush out the seams. You can do this by either using a needle or a bear brush. Go around the seams of the bear using a brush or pick out the hair using a needle until it looks nice. Sometimes you need to adjust the position of the arms and legs. Just twist and bend them until they reach the right positions. Finally, find the perfect ribbon for your bear and don't forget to give it a hug.

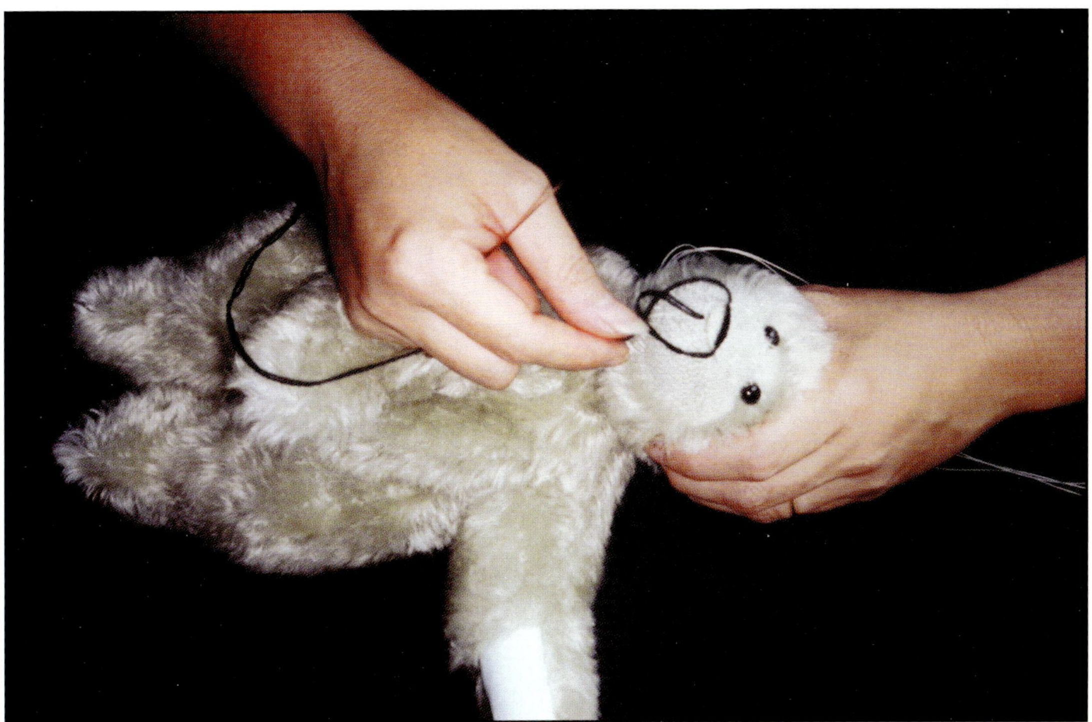

Putting on the nose. Do not make a knot in the thread. First outline the nose.

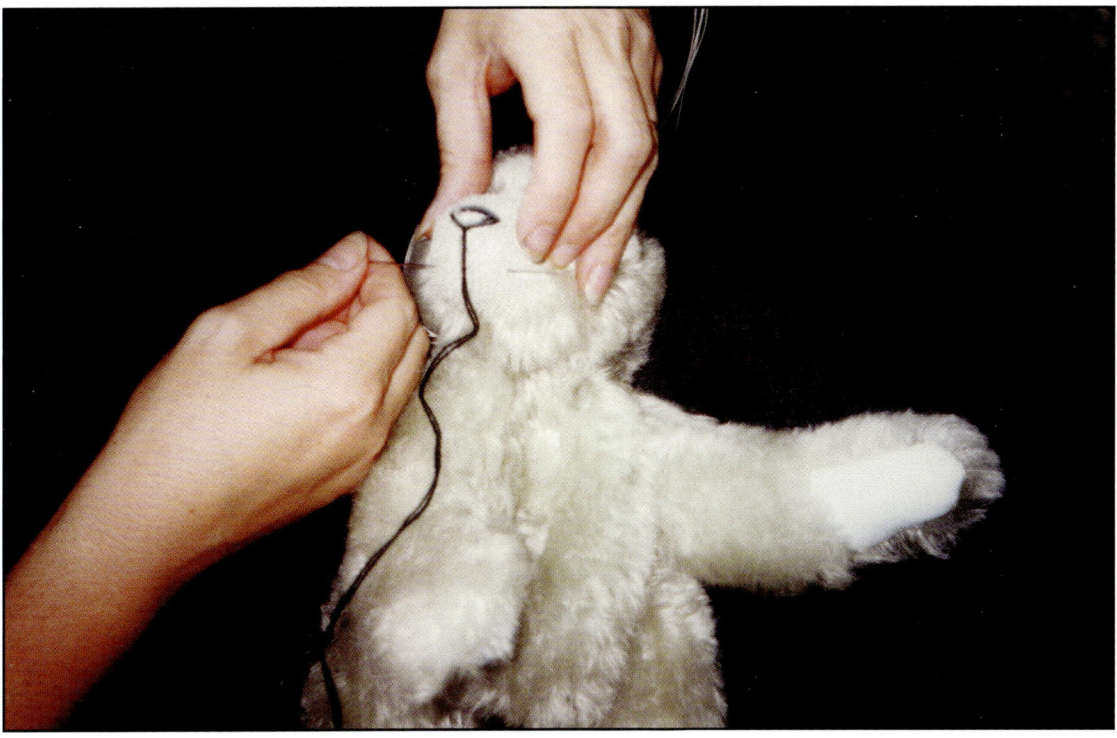

Next I place where I would like the mouth to be.

97

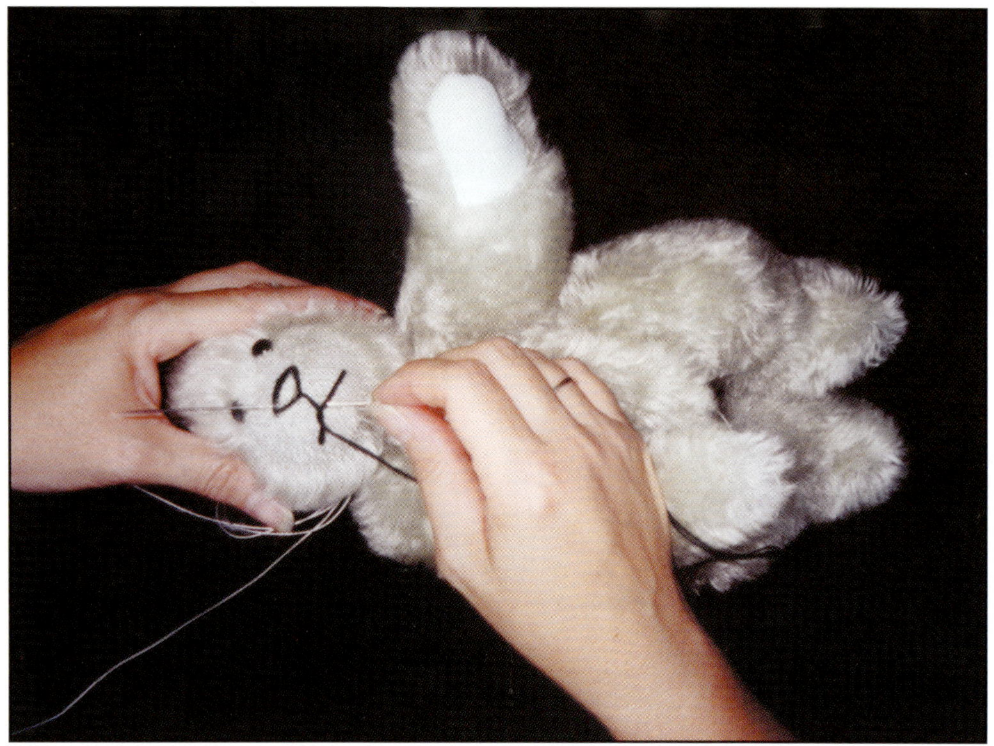

I secure the mouth into place.

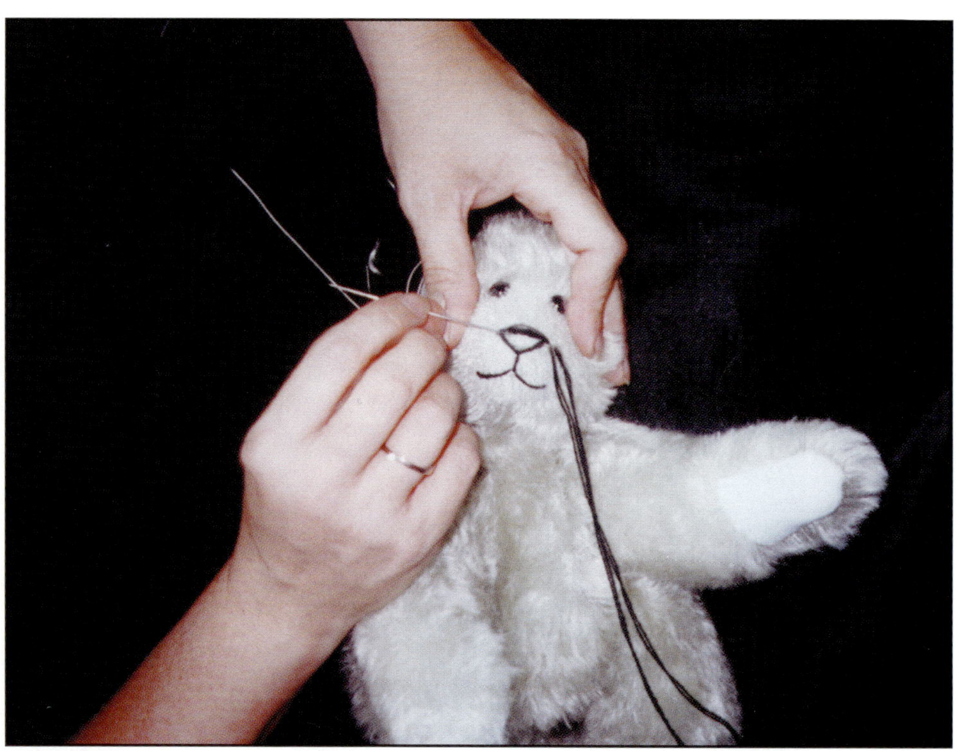

Then I go and fill in the nose with the embroidery stitch

Baby Flash Fire

Pattern

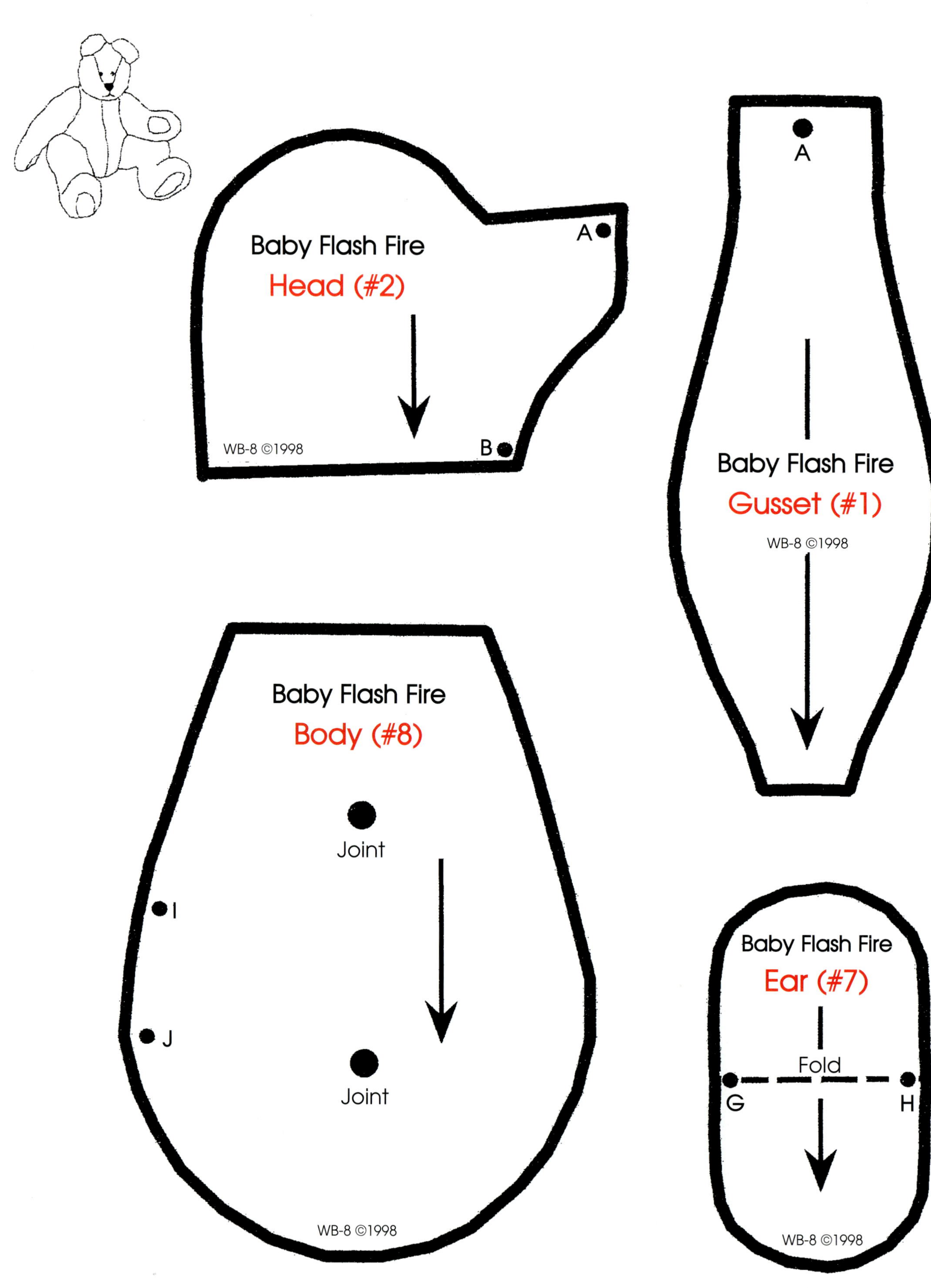

Baby Flash Fire
Head (#2)
A
B
WB-8 ©1998

Baby Flash Fire
Gusset (#1)
A
WB-8 ©1998

Baby Flash Fire
Body (#8)
Joint
I
J
Joint
WB-8 ©1998

Baby Flash Fire
Ear (#7)
Fold
G
H
WB-8 ©1998

Baby Flash Fire
Arm (#4)
Slit
Fold
C
D
WB-8 ©1998
Baby Flash Fire
Paw Pad (#3)
C
D
WB-8 ©1998
Baby Flash Fire
Foot Pad
(#6)
WB-8 ©1998
F
E
Baby Flash Fire
Leg (#5)
Slit
Fold
E
F
E
WB-8 ©1998

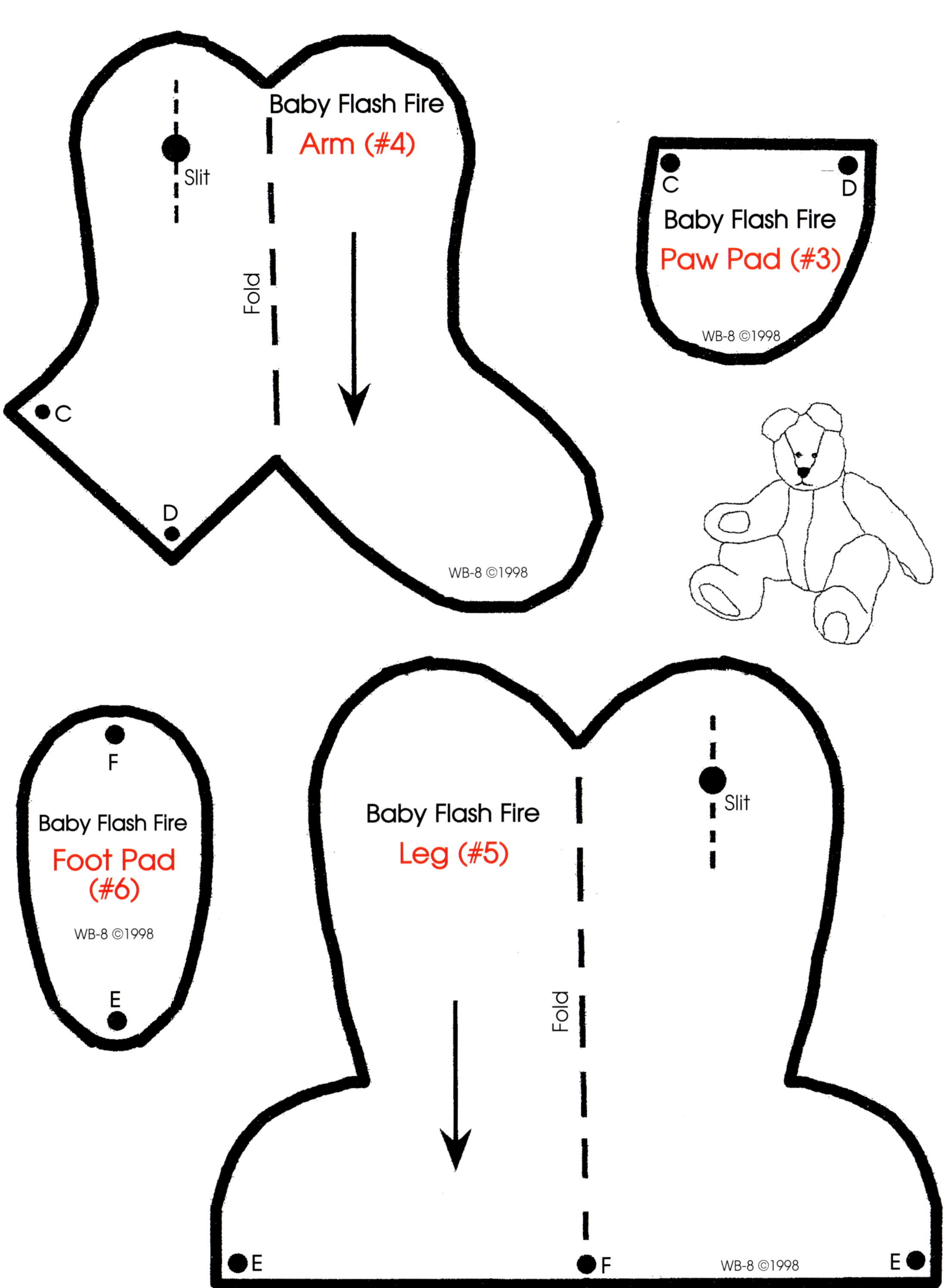

101

Some Bear Over the Rainbow

Pattern

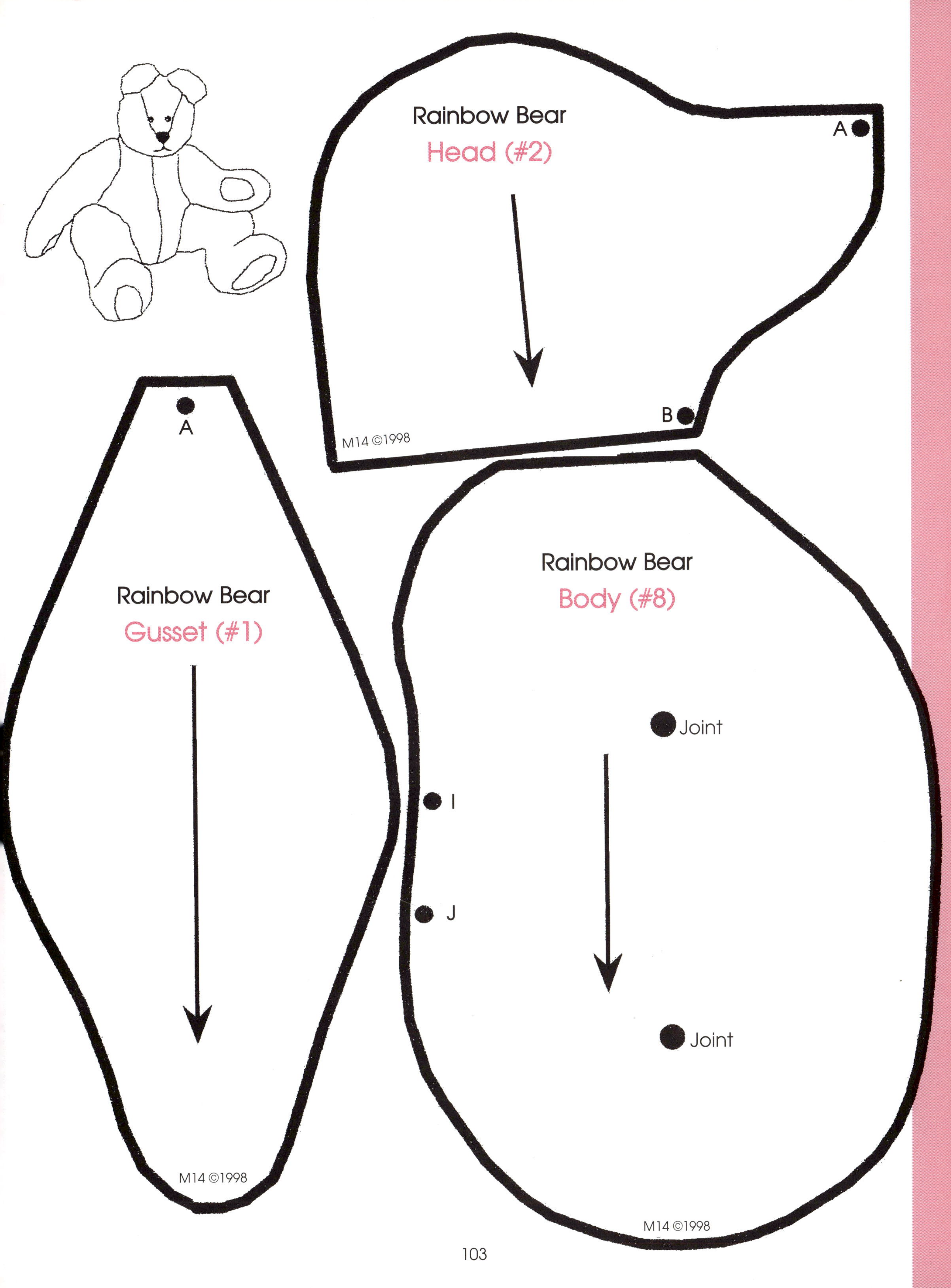

Rainbow Bear
Head (#2)
A
B
M14 ©1998
Rainbow Bear
Gusset (#1)
A
M14 ©1998
Rainbow Bear
Body (#8)
Joint
I
J
Joint
M14 ©1998

Rainbow Bear
Ear (#7)

G — Fold — H

M14 ©1998

Fold, pin and sew 1/4" of the seam

Slit

Rainbow Bear
Arm (#4)

Fold

C

D

M14 ©1998

C — D

Rainbow Bear
Paw Pad (#3)

M14 ©1998

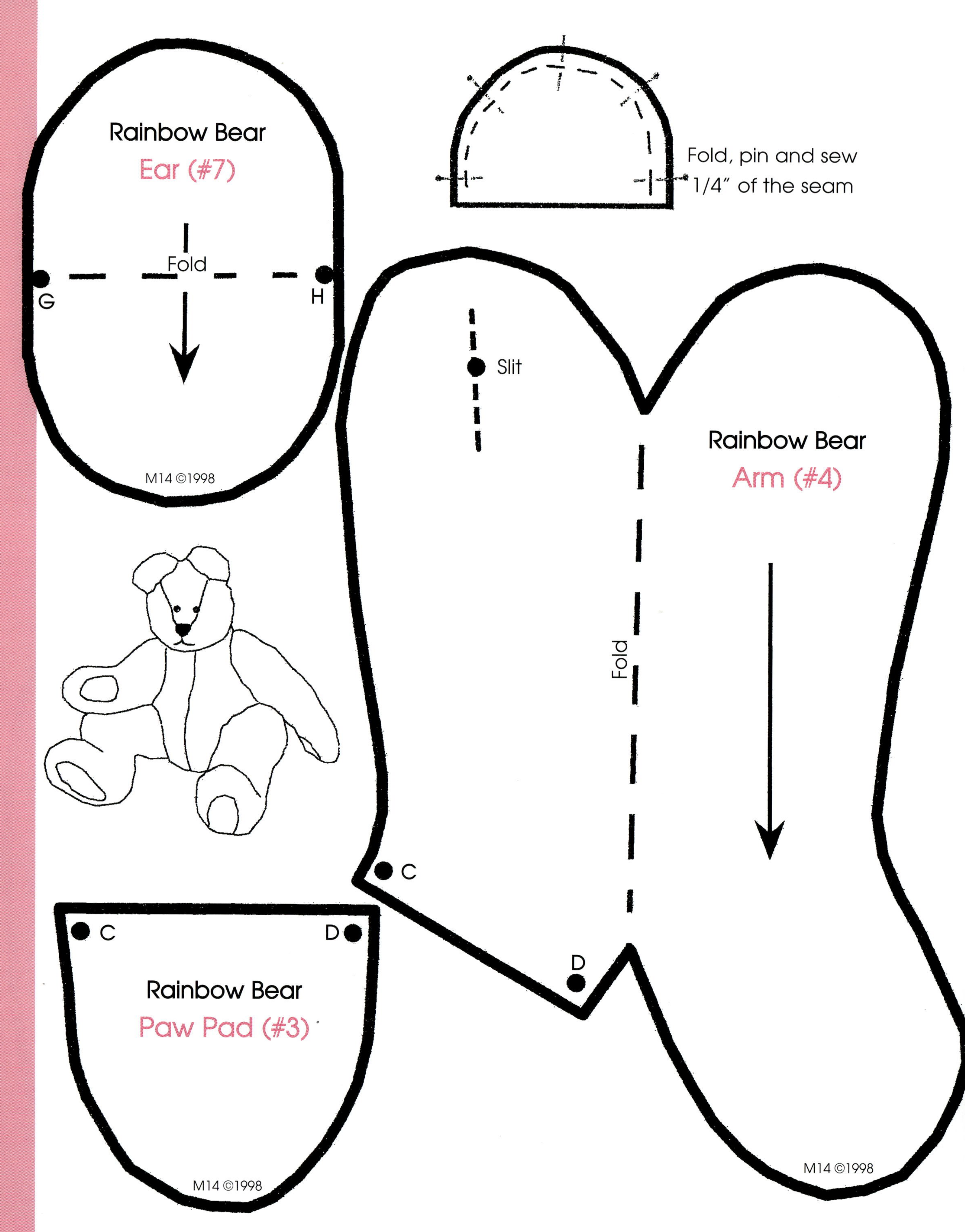

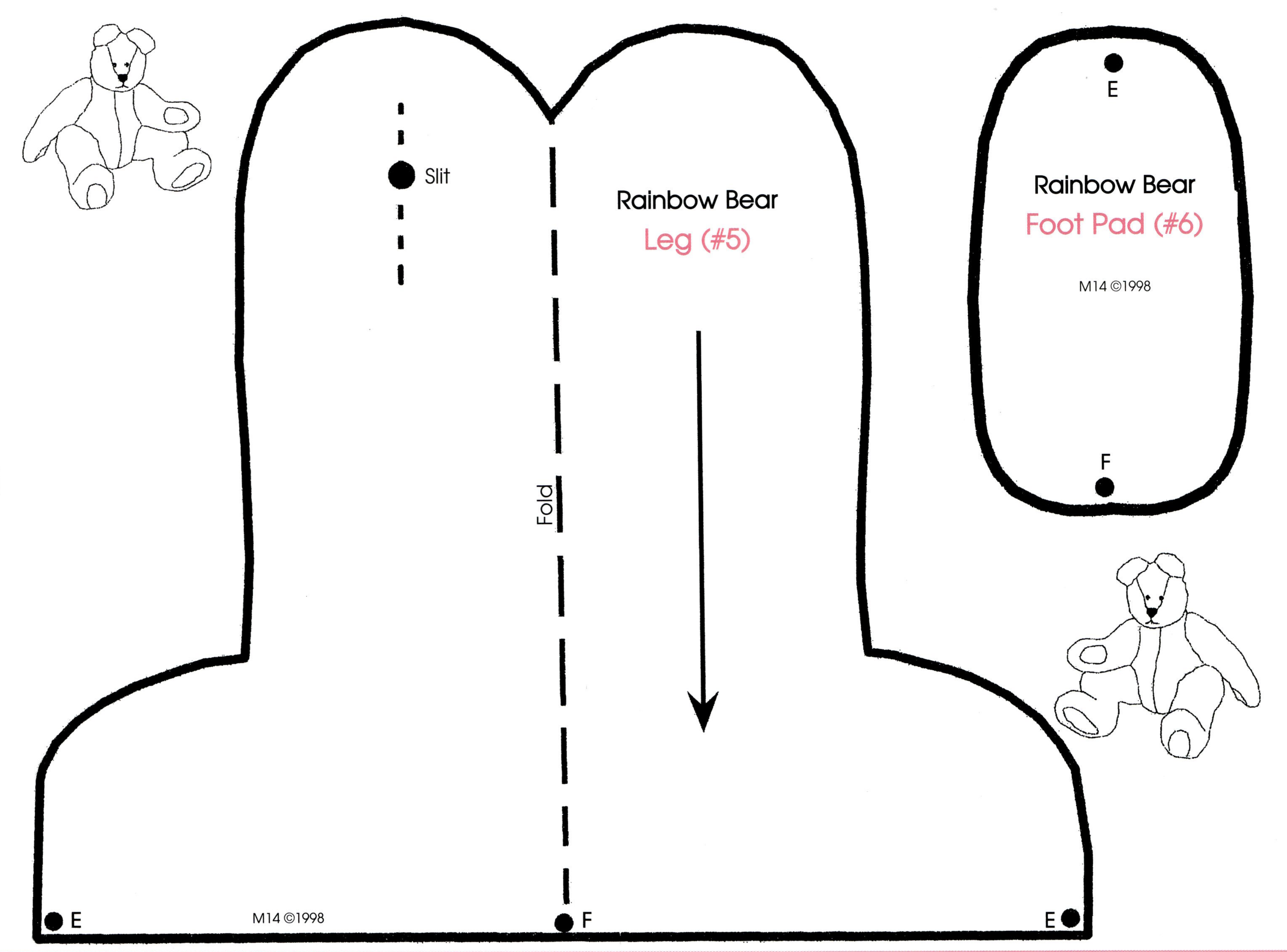
Slit
Rainbow Bear
Leg (#5)
Rainbow Bear
Foot Pad (#6)
M14 ©1998
E
F
Fold
E
M14 ©1998
F
E

Sweet Baby Cheeks

Pattern

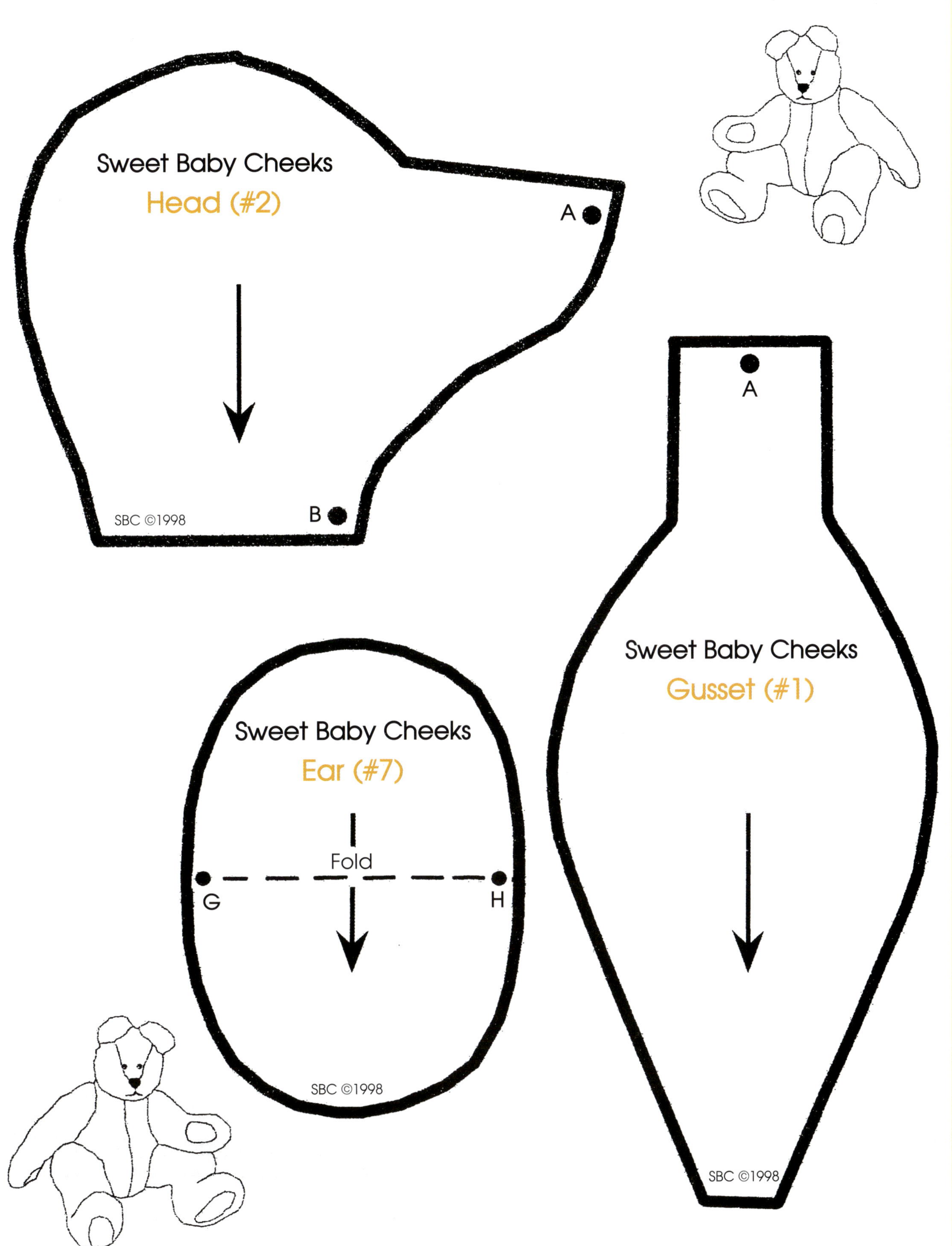

Sweet Baby Cheeks
Head (#2)
A
B
SBC ©1998
Sweet Baby Cheeks
Ear (#7)
Fold
G
H
SBC ©1998
Sweet Baby Cheeks
Gusset (#1)
A
SBC ©1998

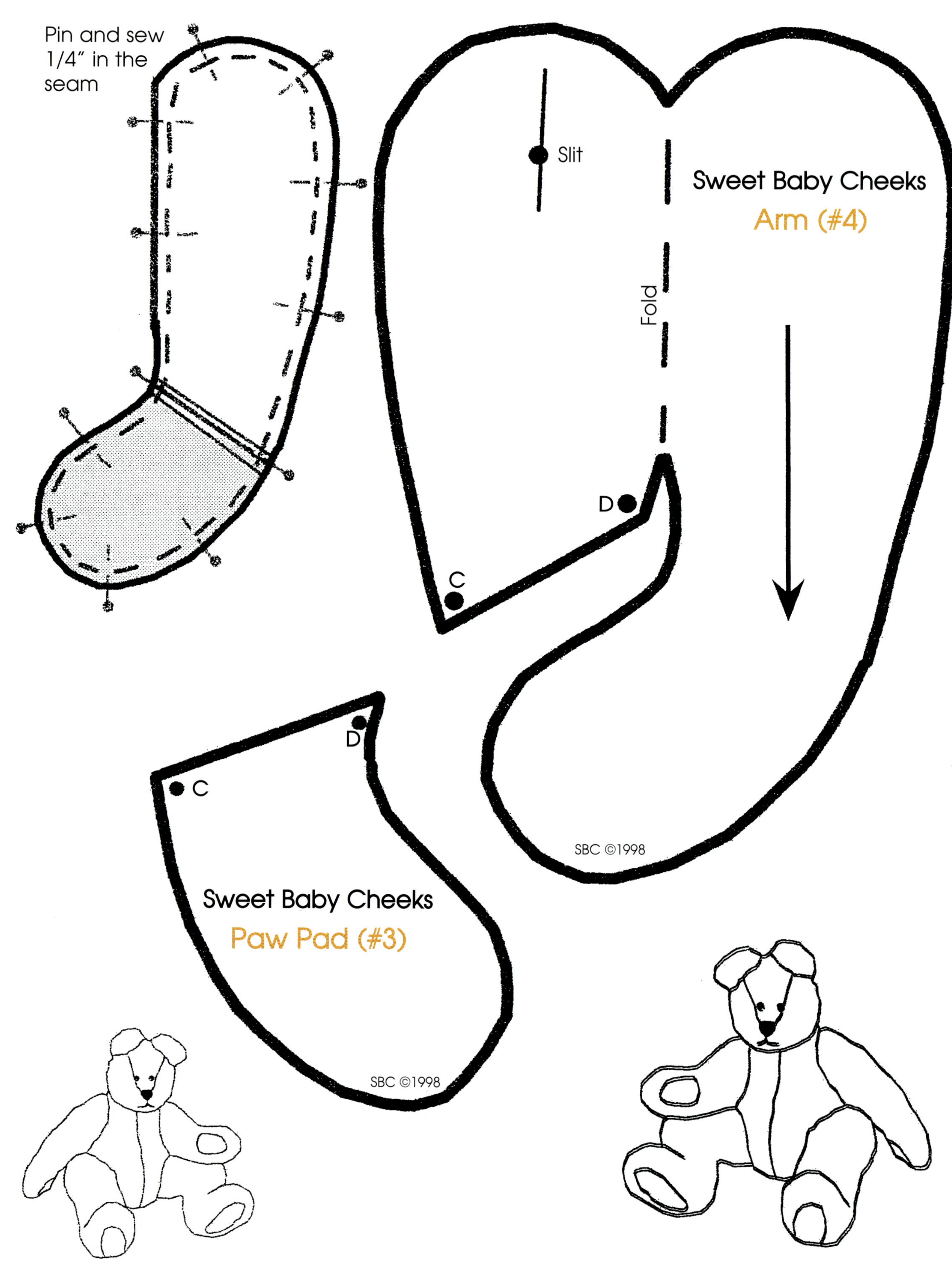

Pin and sew 1/4" in the seam
Slit
Sweet Baby Cheeks
Arm (#4)
Fold
D
C
SBC ©1998
D
C
Sweet Baby Cheeks
Paw Pad (#3)
SBC ©1998

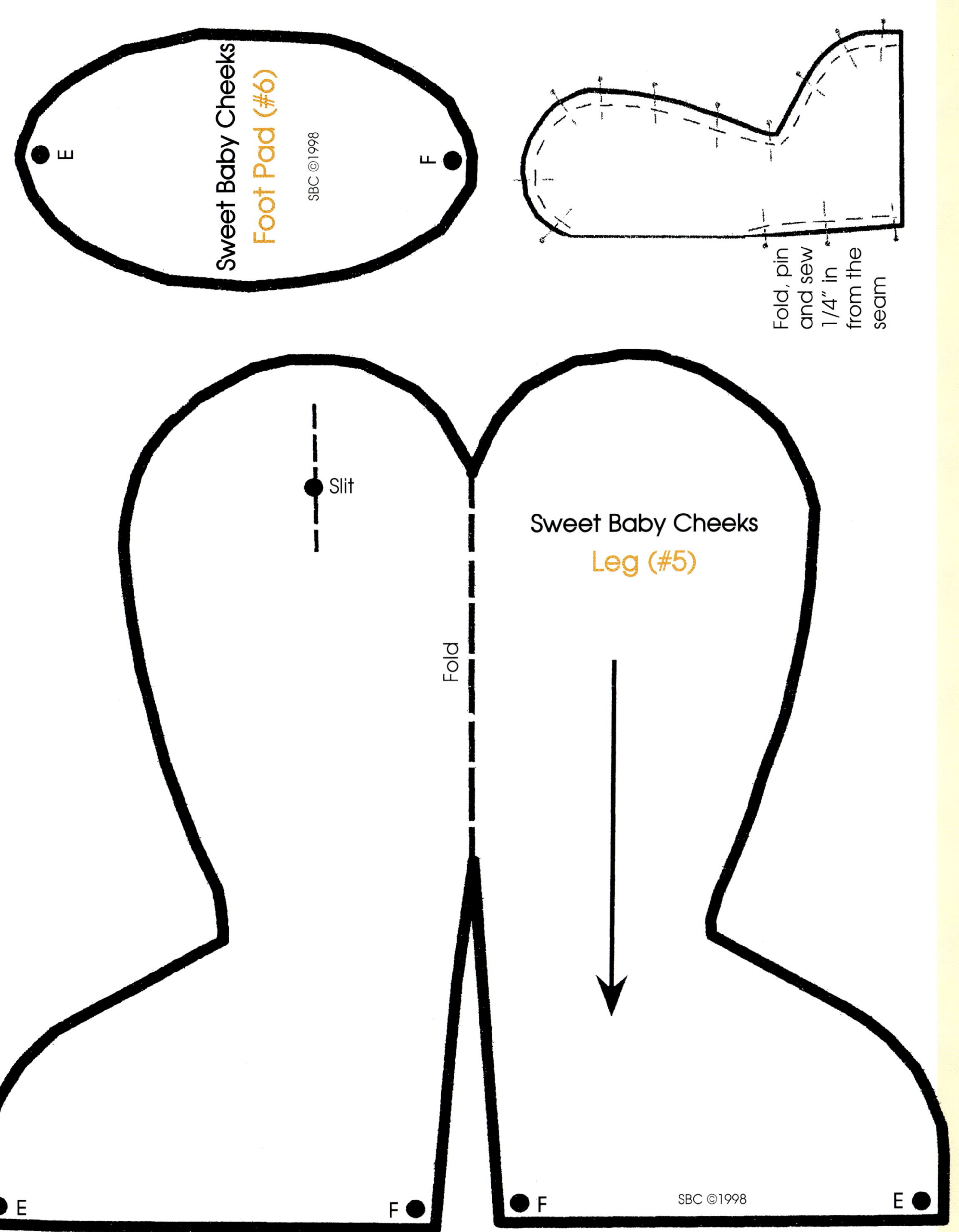

Sweet Baby Cheeks
Foot Pad (#6)
SBC ©1998
E
F
Fold, pin and sew 1/4" in from the seam
Slit
Fold
Sweet Baby Cheeks
Leg (#5)
E
F
F
SBC ©1998
E

Glossary

alpaca - llama hair

colorfast - making sure the color will not come out of the fabric

crocking - when color rubs off of one piece of fabric onto another

crowding - putting too much fabric on the dye pot so that dye cannot penetrate the entire length evenly

dry weight - the weight of the fabric before wetting

dye pot - the container used to mix the dye solution on which the fabric is dyed

fading - when the color becomes lighter due to washing and drying or exposure to light

felting - the process of making felt from the different types of wool

matting - the process of felting causes the materials to mat

mohair - angora goat hair

running/bleeding - when colors from one area of fabric permeate into another area of color

wool - sheep hair

REFERENCES

Winey Bears
Specializes in:
- Handmade artist collectible teddy bears
- Design & Production of limited editions
- Restoration and repairs of stuffed collectibles and toys
- Kits and Videos available

Winey Bears
P.O. Box 63
Birchrunville, PA 19421
phone: 610-827-0166
www.wineybears.com
email: sallywiney@msn.email.com

Sally Winey's Collectors Club
A collectors club where members receive a free Sally Winey "Friendship" Bear ($20 Value), a certificate, membership card and button, the Club Gazette issued quarterly, and special discount opportunities.
Attn: Pauline Ritthaler
Sally Winey Collector's Club
1212 S. Naper Blvd., #119
Naperville, Illinios 60566

Supplies

Edinburgh Imports Inc.
Specializes in:
- Imported German mohair
- Teddy bear making supplies

Edinburgh Imports Inc.
P.O. Box 340 Dept. F
Newbury Park, CA 91319-0340
phone: 805-376-1700
fax: 805-376-1711
www.edinburgh.com
email: rblock@edinburgh.com

Intercal Trading Group
Specializes in:
- Imported English mohair
- Teddy bear making supplies

Intercal Trading Group
Department G
1760 Monrovia Ave., Suite A-17
Costa Mesca, CA 92627
phone: 949-645-9396
fax: 949-645-5471
www.intercaltg.com

Design Master's Spray Paints
Paint for painting the material
Design Masters
P.O. Box 601
Boulder, CO 80306

Rit Dye
Dye for coloring the material
Best Foods Specialty Products
7000 Sylvan Avenue
Englewood Cliff, NJ 07632

Magazines

Teddy Bear and Friends Magazine
Advertising, marketing, and articles on artist and collectible teddy bears.
Subscription Info: 800-829-3340 in US and Canada
949-446-6914 Foreign

Mary Beth's Bean Bag Monthly
Advertising, marketing, and articles in the manufactured beans and plush industry.
Subscription Info: 800-310-7047 (9am-5pm)
fax: 281-261-5999
Mary Beth's Bean Bag Club
www.beanbagworld.net

Wholesale Locations

Cascade Toy
The toy manufacturer with the Sally Winey plush line.
Cascade Toy
P.O. Box 1425
North Bend, WA 98045
phone: 425-888-4600
fax: 425-888-9699
phone: 800-882-8087
www.cascadetoy.com

Classic Collecticritters
Specializes in:
Licensed limited editions of Winey Bears.
Classic Collecticritters
315 South Coast Highway 101, Suite U-12
Encinitas, CA 92024
phone: 760-602-0741
fax: 760-804-0970
www.collecticritters.com

Planet Plush
The bean manufacturing company that carries a line of Sally Winey designed beans.
For Authorized Dealer inquiries contact:
Angie Savatti at: 416-513-9464
www.planetplush.com

News Websites

Beanie Mom
A website for news in the bean and bear industry. It has updates of Winey Bears news.
www.beaniemom.com

Ms. Janie's Collectors Studio
A website for news in the bean and bear industry. It has updates of Winey Bears news.
www.msjanie.com

Retail Websites

Grumble Bears
Teddy Bear Artist retailer on the Web.
www.grumblebears.com

Hand Crafted Beauties
Teddy Bear Artist retailer on the Web.
www.handcraftedbeauties.com

Retail Stores

Contact Winey Bears to find the Winey Bear Retailer in your area.
phone: 610-827-0166

Winey Bears
P.O. Box 63
Birchrunville, PA 19421

The Cambridge Bear Shoppe
2937 Cambridge Rd.
Honey Brook, PA 19344
phone: 610-273-7889

Campbell's Collectibles
10971 Four Season's Plaza
Crown Point, IN 46307
phone: 219-988-3615

Miss Caroline's Country Market
1063 Rt. 97
Waterford, PA 16441
phone: 814-796-3028

Noah's Ark
5603 Cambridge Dr.
Fredricksburg, VA 22407
phone: 540-898-6887

Timeless Treasures
2920 Moonstation Rd.
Kennesaw, GA 30144
phone: 678-290-0808

Bears, Bears and Collectibles
8045 N. Vineyard Ave.
Rancho Cucamonga, CA 91730
phone: 909-944-0923

Machechal & Company, Inc.
13366 Beach Ave.
Marina del Rey, CA 90292
www.TeddyBearWonderland.com

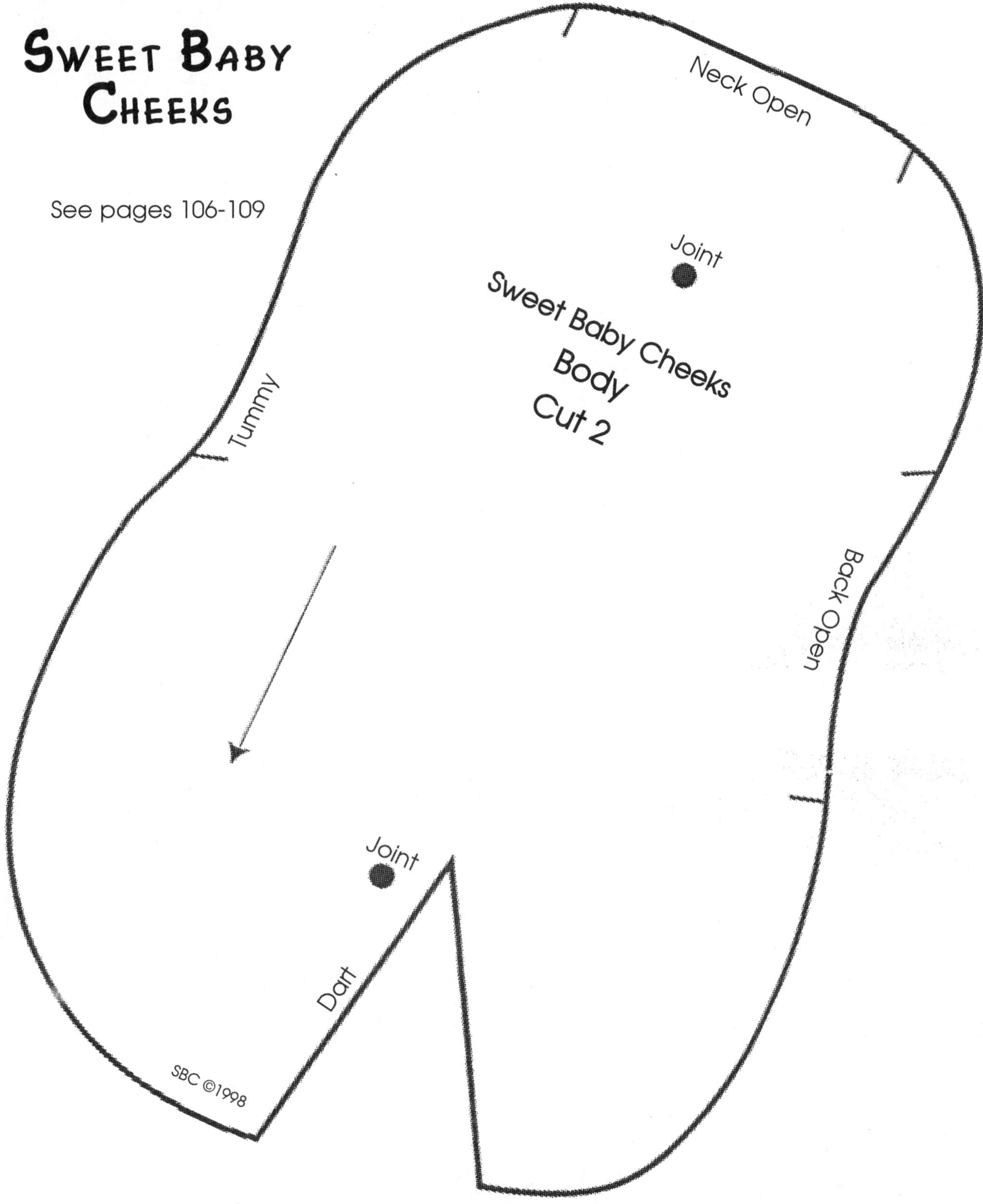

SWEET BABY CHEEKS

See pages 106-109

Rainbow Bears To Make & Collect
by Sally Winey
Hobby House Press, Inc., 1 Corporate Drive, Grantsville, Maryland 21536
1-800-554-1447 • www.hobbyhouse.com
©2000 by Sally Winey

ISBN: 0-87588-593-4